Table of Contents

GREENHOUSE GARDENING

Introduction

Hydroponics is used as a controlled agriculture system for growing out of season crops, for producing crops in areas that are less suited for growing crops, and in areas where the water supply cannot support conventional farming. Research centers also take up hydroponics to grow crops they need to study plant nutrition, plant breeding, and plant diseases because the conditions under which the crops are grown can be regulated as desired. Almost all plants can be grown using hydroponics.

When crops are grown in this way, they use up 50% less land and 90% less water when contrasted with traditional crop-growing methods. However, the yields from the crops are 4 times more, and the crop growth rate is twice as fast when using hydroponics. This is possible because the crops have everything they would need, at the right concentrations.

In place of the soil used in typical agriculture, the farmer or gardener roots the plants in compounds like vermiculite, clay pellets or rock wool. All substances used must be inert so that they do not introduce any new elements into the plant's environment. The solution of water and nutrients is then poured over the support material so that the plant can feed into it.

One primary advantage that hydroponics offer over traditional crop husbandry methods is that when the systems are carefully manipulated and the growing environment properly managed, in terms of the quantity of water provided, pH levels and the combination and concentration of the nutrients. When these conditions are looked into carefully, the crops grow faster. There is less waste in regards to the consumption of resources. There is also less reliance on fertilizers, pesticides and other potentially harmful products used in conventional agriculture.

The development of hydroponics has not only been a response to the current food and resource problems. It is a solution for the future too. Experts say that by 2050, about 80% of all the food produced will be consumed in the cities, which makes it important for the cities to become producers of food. Currently, most cities are the good 'black holes' because all they do is suck in much of it, and at the same time, the cities are the biggest food wasters.

It is easy to see the wastefulness and excessive nature of normal food production in comparison to hydroponics. To supply food to the urban areas, producers need to produce it in large amounts and to transport it there, sometimes, across vast distances, before it is introduced into the market. From the initial step of production, harvesting, packaging, and shipping, the food takes up large amounts of resources that could be saved and re-used elsewhere. People are involved, pollution-causing fuels, buildings, and other resources, and this is wasteful, in comparison to what hydroponics entails.

As the world's population is getting close to 7.5 billion and the demand for more food increasing just as fast, with emphasis on resource-intensive foods, it is clear that farming needs to be done even in the cities, and even so, more productively.

Hydroponic Will Soon Take The Bulk Of Agricultural Production
Although the vast majority of plants are grown using soil, the use of hydroponics has been rising. Thanet Earth, the largest greenhouse complex in the United Kingdom, took up controlled-environment agriculture to produce approximately 225 million tomato fruits, 16 million peppers and 13 million cucumbers in 2013. This production was 12, 11 and 8 percent of Britain's total annual production of these crops, respectively. Thanet Earth made this record-breaking production with only four greenhouses and was hoping to add to this number.

In 2015, it was estimated that hydroponic farming has grown, and was worth $21.4 billion, with an expected annual growth of 7%. It would seem that hydroponics farming is changing slowly, but steadily.

Besides the changing dynamics of farming itself, other outside forces are pushing for the change, advocating for more controlled-agriculture, to boost food production. The earth's population is one key factor. It is expected that by 2050, the global population will have risen by a staggering 3billion persons, and more than 80 percent of the total population will be dwelling in the urban centers. Since we are already using the available farming areas, the arid regions too will need to be converted to production centers, and the way to do this is by introducing hydroponic farming in these areas.

One of the more popular methods is vertical urban farming where hydroponic farms are stacked one over another, in buildings, even in tall skyscrapers. This would be an ideal solution, especially when much of the land is taken up to house the large urban population. It would also place the farms strategically, right where the fresh produce is needed. Singapore and Michigan are already constructing these vertical gardens, and south London is also placing the disused bomb shelters into good use.

Interestingly, as man ventures further and further away from the Earth, NASA is looking into creating hydroponic farms in space to feed the astronauts. The research has been taking place at the University of Arizona, where scientists are looking into the possibility of creating a closed-loop system that will feel carbon dioxide and human waste into a hydroponic farm, which will possibly lead to the creation of oxygen, food, and water.

You could look forward to seeing some space-grown tomatoes in the future, but good luck with the human waste growing material.

How Hydroponics Works

We have already established that in contrast to traditional agriculture where the soil provides support to the plant, allowing it to remain upright and providing a supply of nutrients, in hydroponics plants have artificial support and a solution containing all the required nutrients is provided. The idea behind the hydroponic setup is simple. It is thought that environmental factors often limit plant growth, and therefore, by providing a solution that contains nutrients to the plant's roots, the gardener provides a constant optimal supply of nutrients and water. The nutritional efficiency makes a plant live up to its potential by making it more productive.

The nutrient-rich solution is delivered in a number of ways:

- In the first, the plants are placed in an inert substance, as mentioned earlier, and its roots are occasionally flooded with the solution.

- Secondly, the plants could be placed on the inert substances and the solution rained on the plant using a solution dripper.

- The third option places the plants on a film that slightly slopes, and this allows the solution to trickle down to the roots of the plants

- The fourth way has the plant and its roots suspended in the air, and the roots are occasionally sprayed with the solution mist.

All the methods described above use machines to do one thing or another, either by the use of a mister, or using a pump to deliver the solution from its storage area. The solution must also be aerated so that the roots get the oxygen they require once the solution comes on. Plants need the energy to absorb the minerals in the solution, and this absorption process requires energy, which is made possible by respiration.

Is It Hard?

Certainly, setting up and maintaining a hydroponics system can be quite a difficult task. This is because the plants need an assortment of nutrients, and each species' optimal amount of nutrients varies. In addition, each plant's nutritional requirements will change as it goes through various developmental stages. Local conditions such as the hardness of the water to be used also matters a lot.

It is also a fact that some nutrients are absorbed into the plant much faster than others which can cause a buildup of some ions in the solution, hence a change of the solution's pH. Once the pH is affected, the absorption of other nutrients by the plant is hindered because the uptake of some nutrients is pH-dependent, and because the excess availability of some nutrients prevents the uptake of others. For example, when the ammonia content is very high, the calcium uptake decreases, and on the other hand, too much calcium reduces the absorption of magnesium.

Another critical aspect to be careful about is that some elements react with one another, and form compounds that are difficult to absorb, which means that they have to be provided at different times.

With the above different variations, a hydroponic farmer must have a good grasp of the requirements of plants and the interaction of nutrients with each other, and with the plants themselves. They must carefully monitor the solutions they provide to the plants and check to see the changes in concentration that could come about. The alternative option is for the farmer to invest in an automated hydroponics system, which is quite expensive, to run the process on his or her behalf.

Farmers are also obliged to take great care of the solutions they are using to keep them from contamination by unwanted substances. Most choose to enclose the hydroponics project inside a greenhouse or a building to ensure that they alone have control of what is going on in the systems. This limitation also gives the farmers the liberty to optimize on the environmental influences of the plant, such as the light, carbon dioxide exposure and the temperatures, all to maximize the yields received.

This means that hydroponics is just not about growing crops without using soil; it also means that the farmer has absolute control of the plants and their growing process, at least.

The Science Behind Hydroponics

As a rule, plants need next to no to develop. They can subsist on a straightforward mix of water, daylight, carbon dioxide and mineral supplements from the dirt. Plants can change light vitality into concoction vitality to frame sugars that enable them to develop and continue themselves. These supplements can be normally happening in soil and are found in most business manures. Notice that the dirt itself isn't required for plant development: the plant essentially needs the minerals from the dirt. This is the essential reason behind hydroponics - every one of the components required for plant development is equivalent to with conventional soil-based cultivating. Hydroponics basically removes the dirt necessities.

There are a few distinct sorts of hydroponic frameworks, however, each depends on similar beginning ideas. Here, we'll inspect each type, find how and why it's utilized and see which sorts of plants react best to every strategy.

Back and forth movement Systems require a medium, for example, perlite, which fills no need other than to give solidness to the plant's underlying foundations. The plant gets no supplements from the medium itself. Back and forth movement frameworks incorporate a plate in which the plant is set in a medium; underneath the plate in a different holder is a store containing water and mineral arrangements. The water from the store is intermittently siphoned up into the plate. This floods the plate and enables the plants to ingest water and supplements. Bit by bit, the water depletes once more into the repository because of gravity. Back and forth movement frameworks work best with little plants like herbs and are normally utilized in smaller hydroponic arrangements, for example, those in the home.

Supplement Film Technique (NFT) is a water-based framework that requires no dirt or mediums. They're assembled utilizing wooden channels, which bolster polyethylene film liners. Plants, for example, tomatoes and cucumbers are set on the channels, and the supplement improved water is siphoned to the high finish of each channel. The channels slant down, and water is gathered toward the conclusion to be siphoned back through the framework and reused. Just plants with enormous built uproot frameworks will work with this procedure.

Trickle Systems are set up indistinguishable from a back and forth movement framework, despite the fact that rather than water being siphoned through one enormous cylinder, it's siphoned through numerous little cylinders and channels onto the highest point of the plants. This framework is perfect for plants that don't yet have a created root framework, and as a recurring pattern framework, works best with smaller plants.

Wick Systems are like rhythmic movement frameworks in that they're medium-based. Plants are set into a plate loaded up with a medium, for example, perlite or rockwool. At the base of each root, a nylon rope is set, which is permitted to dangle openly, reaching out past the base of the plate. The whole plate is then set over a repository. The nylon ropes retain the water and supplements, wicking them up to the plant's underlying foundations. This framework is alluring in light of the fact that it requires no siphons or other gear to be bought.

Chapter 1: Difference between Hydroponic Gardening and Traditional Gardening

Both hydroponic and soil gardening methods have their advantages and disadvantages, and as you continue to read this book you will discover that not all plants are suitable for hydroponic systems. However, a surprising number are, including many that you would not think could be grown without soil, such as potatoes and carrots.

Areas Where Hydroponic Gardening is Better Than Soil Gardening

Hydroponics save space

Hydroponics takes up very little space, and you can grow an indoor hydroponic system in your room. Besides, the absence of soil means root systems are short, so you can grow plants closer together and save space.

Weather free growing

The weather can be the biggest hindrance to growing anything outside. In a hydroponic system, you have full control over the environment and are growing indoors, so there is no weather to upset your growing plans!

Lower water use

Growing in soil is surprisingly water inefficient, so in an area where water is expensive or scarce, it is very costly to grow vegetables. However, a hydroponic system, despite being made up mainly of water, using significantly less water than growing in soil because it is more efficient in its use of water.

Fewer pests

Have you ever lost your crop to pests? Had caterpillars devoured your cauliflower? Pests are a significant problem when growing outside and mean either companion planting, using a pesticide, or accepting you will lose a portion of your crop. Hydroponic plants are grown indoors in an enclosed environment, so the chances of pests are meager. Of course, there is the chance that you will find the occasional pest, but as you are regularly checking the system, you tend to spot any pest problems very early on before they cause much damage.

Fewer diseases

It is very frustrating to lose your entire crop because of a disease. Although you can spray for many conditions, there are just as many for which there is no treatment. As you are growing indoors, diseases are very uncommon. Practicing proper hygiene and quarantining new plants before introducing them to the system will help to reduce the risk of illness to virtually zero.

Fewer artificial chemicals

Although there is a significant movement away from the use of chemicals in gardening, they are still introduced into your garden through the wind and rain. However, some gardeners will use pesticides and artificial fertilizers. Growing hydroponically, you use far fewer chemicals, which is a huge benefit for many gardeners.

No digging

A distaste of many gardeners is the need to dig over the soil, hence the popularity of systems such as the no-dig system involving layering compost and cardboard. There is no digging involved in hydroponic gardening, as there is no soil.

Rapid maturing crops

When you grow plants hydroponically, they mature far faster than if they are grown in soil or even in a greenhouse. Typically, plants will develop in three-quarters of the usual growing time, but some can mature in up to half the time. Obviously, this means you can get more crops per year, and when combined with the next point, has significant benefits for commercial growers.

Reliable & predictable yields

Growing hydroponically produces very reliable yields because you are not reliant on the vagrancies of the weather. Yields are typically much higher because of the consistent growing conditions, producing up to double the yield.

Lower labor requirement

Because there is less work involved, you just check the pH and nutrient levels regularly, there is a lot less labor involved.

Higher nutritional content

Scientific analysis of hydroponically grown vegetables has shown that they contain up to 50% more vitamins and minerals than vegetables grown in soil.

Obviously, this means some health benefits and is a big advantage for many growers.

Hydroponics uses less water
When grown via a hydroponic system, the plants need less water. When you water plants that are in the soil, often the water seeps into the ground, and some water also gets evaporated. But the hydroponic system is much more water-efficient, and you use 70 to 80% less water.

Hydroponics systems lower, pests, weeds, and diseases
With traditional soil planting the risk of pests, weeds, and diseases increases; but a hydroponic system deals with this problem almost completely.

Hydroponic systems grow plants faster
Hydroponic systems grow plants twice as fast as traditional methods, which means you get more harvests every year. The growing cycle is much more efficient because the plants get everything it needs.

Hydroponics let you adjust nutrient content for different plants
Hydroponics allows you to tweak and adapt nutrients for every plant.

Areas Where Soil Gardening is Better

Lower initial cost
The initial cost of hydroponics can be quite expensive. But soil gardening has a lower initial price.

No need to use electricity
A light source is needed in several hydroponic gardening techniques. Also, some systems use power to aerate the roots.

Less risk of bacteria and mold growth
In a hydroponics system, plants grow in a very moist environment. If precautions are not taken, then there is a susceptible risk of mold and bacteria growth.

Now you know the main differences between the traditional soil growing method and the hydroponics system. In the next chapter, we will explore more in-depth the process of hydroponic gardening.

Chapter 2: Types of Hydroponic Gardening

If we want to become hydroponic gardeners, the first thing we need to do is understand what options are available to us. This way we can choose a method that has advantages and disadvantages that are properly in line with what we are looking for. This means, for example, if we don't want to risk clogs, we could avoid using methods that involve pumps. However, if we live in an area where we have a hard time controlling the amount of light in our environment, we might find ourselves looking to a system that uses a pump rather than one of the simpler ones like a deep-water culture in which light regulation is also important.

Each of these systems offers unique advantages and disadvantages from which we can choose. But this does not mean that one particular system is better than another. Like most things in life, the choice of which hydroponic system to use should be based on your schedule, needs and abilities. For this reason, I won't be extolling the virtues of any one particular system. Instead, we will look at the most popular systems around to see what their benefits are and what their disadvantages are. This way, you will have the knowledge necessary to choose the type that is right for you.

Hydroponic system

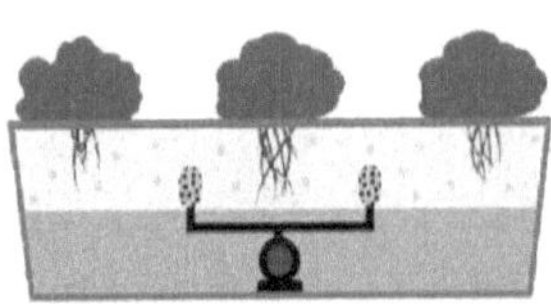

Aeroponics

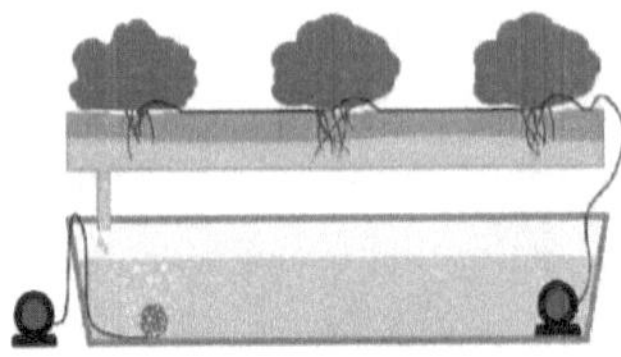

Nutrient film technique

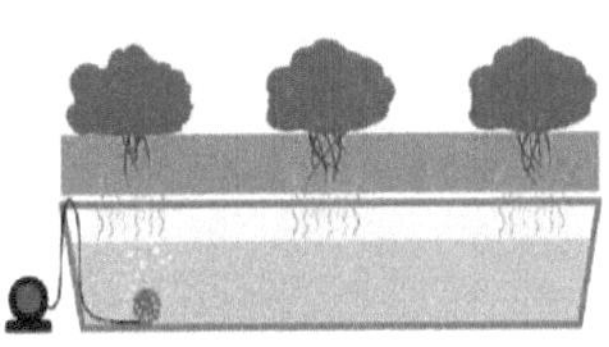

Wick system

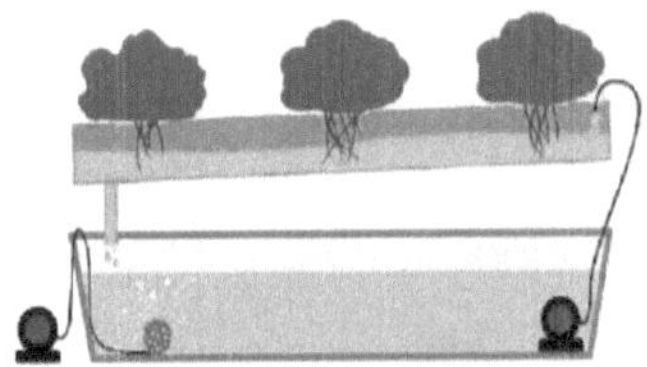

Drip system

Drip System

This system is one of the most popular hydroponic setups but it was actually invented for outdoor gardens in Israel. At its most simplified, the drip system uses a pump to keep a drip of nutrient-rich water feeding our plants. The slow drip, rather than the typical spraying of water we see in gardens, allows for less water to be used.

Typically, a drip system is designed with two key parts. The first is the reservoir of nutrient-rich water that will feed the plants. Above this rests the grow tray in which our plants are potted. A pump is set up in the water and is connected up into the grow tray. From there, each of the plants will be given their own drip line. This means if you are growing four plants in your tray, you would use four drip lines. Sixteen plants, sixteen drip lines. However, because we want to give the growing medium, that substance you use to replace soil (and which we'll be looking at more in chapter three), time to breathe so as not to drown the plants, these drips will use a timer system. The growing medium will slowly release the water back down into the reservoir, creating a closed system.

A drip system offers us great control over the amount of water and nutrients that our plants are getting. With this system, we are able to control the drip both by the quantity and by length. This means if we use too much water in our drip, we can dial it back; or, if our drip is going too long or too short, we can adjust the timers that we are using to experiment until we find the length that's just right. One of the cool things about the drip system is that while it may take a while to set up and get right in the early period, once we have everything in place and know our volumes, the system doesn't require as much overall maintenance (depending on the particular setup) as other methods will. Plus, the materials needed to create a drip system aren't as costly as some of the others.

However, a drip system still uses a pump and a clogged pump can see our gardens decimated in merely a few hours. Of course, this depends on the size of the system. While the drip system is great for large-scale grow operations, it might be too complex for smaller operations. Some drip systems use what is called a non-recovery system which means that the water is not circulated back into the reservoir. These particular systems require less maintenance than systems which do feedback into the reservoir but in doing so they create more waste. This means that regardless of the system we use, we either will require more maintenance or create more waste.

A drip system works well for a variety of herbs and plants ranging from lettuce, onions, and peas to radishes, cucumbers, strawberries and pumpkins. It turns out that these systems actually are fantastic for larger plants. They also work best when making use of a growing medium in which water drains slowly like peat moss or coconut coir.

So, if you are looking to grow larger plants, the drip system is a great choice. Drip systems do require a bit of maintenance and they can be slow to set up at first but once they get going, they offer a high level of control over the growing process that any gardener would love.

Deep Water Culture

Considered the easiest of the hydroponic systems, a deep-water culture uses a reservoir system that the roots of the plants are suspended into. Basically, the plants sit above and instead of dripping water, they just reach down to take the water they want. This makes the system quite easy to set up.

A deep-water culture gets its name from the use of a deep reservoir and from how deep the roots go into the water. Other systems, such as the nutrient film technique, expose the roots of the plants to the air so that they can absorb plenty of oxygen. With this system we set up a grow tray above our reservoir, making sure that the material we use stops light getting through the system to prevent algae from growing inside and messing up the system. From there, the roots are suspended in the water and the water itself is kept oxygenated through the use of an air pump. This is done to keep the roots from drowning in the water.

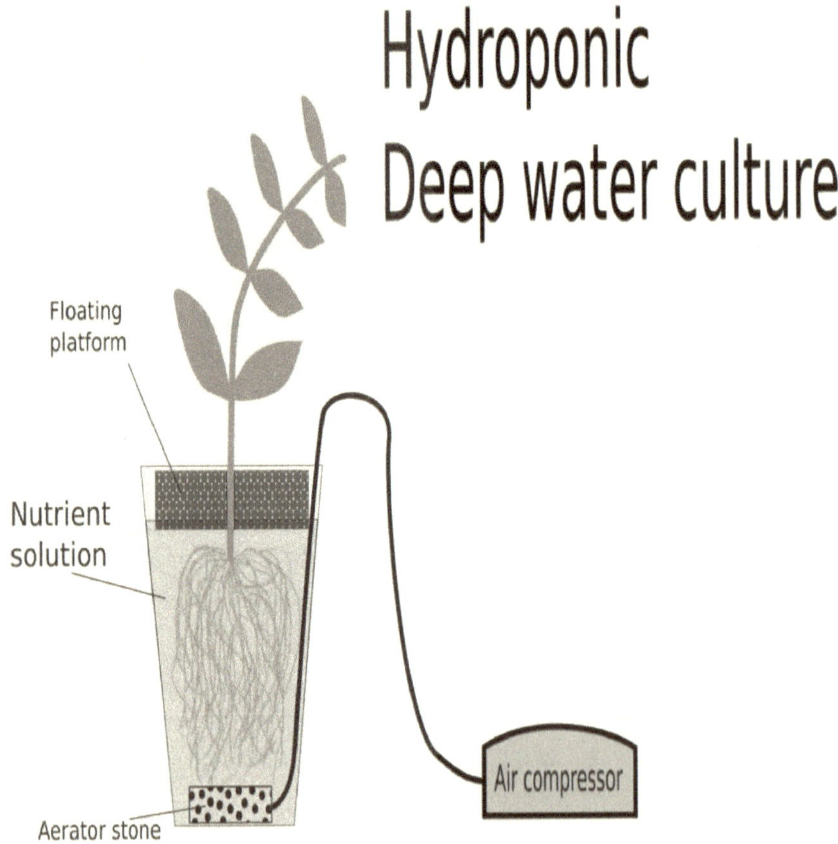

That's pretty much it. It wasn't a joke to say this is among the easiest of the hydroponic setups to get started with.

Deep water cultures are great for this simplicity but it is far from the only benefit that they offer. Because there are so few moving parts in a deep-water culture, they are rather low maintenance. There is an air pump but we don't pump water in this system and so the fear of losing our gardens to a faulty pump is unwarranted here. The easy setup and lower maintenance of these systems make them great for people first getting into hydroponic gardening and wanting to see if the approach is right for them.

However, while the deep-water culture's pump is air-based and so results in fewer blockages, they are still put at risk by power outages. Because the air pump is needed to oxygenate the water, a power outage could see your garden drown. Depending on the size of the system, it can be really tough to maintain proper pH levels in the water. A smaller system is harder to make minor changes in pH level to, as going just a little over or under can make a massive difference at smaller sizes. Finally, it can be really hard to keep a balanced water temperature in these systems as we have to be careful about the exposure of the reservoir to light.

Because of the way the system is set up, with the plants resting above the reservoir, the suitability of crops for the deep-water culture depends on several key factors. The first key is the weight. If the plants we choose are too top-heavy, they can risk toppling over and breaking or even causing the weight of the setup to shift and knocking the top off. That's a disaster nobody wants to experience. The other major point is that we need to choose plants that like water. This means that plants which prefer dry growing conditions won't do very well in a deep-water culture. However, plants such as lettuce which love to soak up water will love this system.

Besides lettuce, some great choices for this system are herbs like basil and greens like kale, collard greens, chard and sorrel. Bok choy and okra also grow well in these systems and offer a variety outside of the traditional vegetables one thinks of as garden veggies.

So if you're looking to grow some water-loving plants, deep water culture is a system that is easy to set up and requires little maintenance. However, we have to be careful about which plants we pick. If they are too top-heavy or prefer dry conditions, the deep-water reservoir isn't for them.

Nutrient Film Technique

With the nutrient film technique, we again use a reservoir of water but this time we are pumping it into a grow tray that has been set up at a slight angle. Doing it this way means that gravity takes care of getting the nutrient-rich water from one end of the tray to the other, where it will then drain back into the reservoir. More information about how we add nutrients to our water is covered in chapter four. Because of the design, this system is best used for plants with a smaller root system. The NFT setup is an active system.

The plants in the NFT system only have the ends of their roots touching the water, so as to keep the roots able to take in precious oxygen which helps growth. Because the system only uses a little water at a time, the plants are never drowned in the water.

Because of the way the plants are positioned, it is very easy to check the roots for disease in the NFT system. The use of a reservoir of water that feeds back into itself reduces the overall waste of water and the design of the system makes it easy to scale the project up or down depending on the size needed. Plus, unlike deep water cultures, it can be fairly easy to get the pH levels right using an NFT setup.

However, the NFT also relies on a pump and so the risk of pump failure and the decimation of your crop is still a possibility that one has to look out for. Because of the way the roots are slotted into the system, they can block up the flow of water. This is why plants with a large root system like carrots aren't a good fit for the NFT system.

Because the roots are not actually in a growing medium like the other systems we looked at, this means that top-heavy plants don't work here either. However, leafy greens like lettuce or fruits like strawberries have found great success growing through an NFT system.

Ebb and Flow

The ebb and flow system get its name from the periodic flooding and draining of nutrient-rich water. It is also known, fittingly, like the flood and drain system. In this system, water floods into the glow tray and soaks the roots of the plants. Then the water drains back down into the reservoir. Flood, drain. Flood, drain. Over and over again, hence the name.

In order to get the system to work properly, we need to set up a pump to flood the grow tray. We set this pump up on a timer rather than let it constantly flood the grow tray and drown the plants. An overflow tube is set up in the grow tray so that the water drains back down into the reservoir.

Depending on how we set it up, we might even include an air pump to make sure that the roots are getting the oxygen that they need.

The nice thing about the ebb and flow system is that it doesn't cost a lot to get started, as the materials aren't particularly hard to get a hold of. This system makes sure our plants are getting enough nutrients without drowning due to the easy to build the structure. Once the system is set up, the hardest part of running it is out of the way. The ebb and flow system is able to run by itself once set up but you should still do maintenance to ensure everything is working properly.

Again, this system uses a pump, which means it can break and broken pumps are notorious for killing off entire gardens. If the structure fails to drain properly, the plants risk drowning and the pH levels in a broken system can be harmful to the plants. This is important to know because this system is prone to breakdowns and so we have to understand which areas a breakdown affects most.

One of the coolest things about the ebb and flow system is that it can be set up to allow just about any kind of plant or vegetable. Not so much the plants that prefer a dry system but the size is not a concern here the way that it was in the nutrient film technique setup. Because of how easy it is to build the structure; we can alter it to fit the needs of our plants rather easily.

Wicking

Out of all of the systems we have and will look at, wicking is the easiest. It is so easy, in fact, that it is often recommended as an entry point to hydroponic gardening. Wicking is a passive system with very few parts, there are no water pumps in a wicked system.

In this system, we once again fill a reservoir with water and keep it beneath a grow tray. This time, however, we don't use tubing to get the water to the plants but rather we set up a wicking material like a rope. This wicking material is placed into the water and threaded up into the grow tray. Our grow tray is filled with a growing medium that is good at absorbing and keeping water because this system works very slowly. Water travels the length of the wick to slowly feed the plants.

This system is great for its simplicity and can serve as an easy way to start getting into hydroponic gardening. It is also an inexpensive system, making it that much easier for the novice grower to invest in. Because there is no pump to break down, this system isn't at risk for a premature death the way pump-based systems are. The lack of a pump also means that this system doesn't use up electricity and it can be refreshing to those worried about the size of their power bill.

However, despite its simplicity, there are still downsides to the wicking system that we have to consider. The system is inefficient at delivering nutrients, so plants that need a lot of water and nutrients aren't a very good match. The system can also see a toxic build-up of nutrients in the growing medium if we are not careful to observe how much water is getting in and being used.

Because of the lower water levels in wicking systems, they are best used for small plants. Lettuce and the smaller of the herbs make good fits for a wicking system but water-hungry plants like tomatoes would absolutely hate a wicking system. For this reason, the wicking system doesn't offer nearly the same variety as other systems. But that lack of variety is made up for by the ease of setup, making wicking a great system for those first trying their hands at hydroponics.

Aeroponics

Saved the most complex for last. Aeroponics does away with the growing medium and instead leaves the roots of the plants exposed to more oxygen and so this system tends to see faster growth.

In this system, the roots of the plants hang down in the open air of the container in which the system is built. At the bottom of the system is our reservoir of nutrient-rich water. However, the roots don't dangle down into the water this time. Instead, we use a pump from the water to spray the plant roots with the nutrient solution. This pump is of course set up on a timer, to ensure we aren't overfeeding the plants. This makes it so that instead of the plant spending energy to grow out longer roots in search of nutrients, the nutrients come to the roots so that the plant can focus its growth elsewhere.

This system is great for producing larger plants since they don't need to focus on root growth. The lack of a growing medium also means that the roots don't need to take hold; we are bringing the nutrients directly onto them. The exposure of the roots to oxygen also helps to promote growth. This means that the aeroponic system is known for producing crops with impressive yields. This system also doesn't require a lot of space can so it can be built to be fairly mobile. Because of the lack of a growing medium, the aeroponic system is rather easy to clean.

We have to make sure to clean it because the constantly wet atmosphere of the system makes for an environment in which bacteria and fungi can thrive. The system is also very much prone to failures related to pumps and loss of power, which we've seen can be a major killer of our hydroponic gardens. The setup of an aeroponic garden also costs more than the other systems and it is the most technical of the hydroponic systems, which means the knowledge to entry is much higher as well. They also require constant supervision to protect against root diseases, fungi and to monitor pH levels and the density of the nutrient solution.

However, this system allows for bigger yields and the system can be used to grow almost any kind of plant. This means that the variety the aeroponic system offers is unparalleled compared to the other systems we have looked at.

Chapter 3: How to Build a Hydroponic System

We have every reason to prepare in good faith for our experiments and, from the very beginning, to eliminate all sources of possible failures. It is extremely annoying to stop a well-started experiment without achieving results, just because not enough attention was paid to some "trifle". About vessels for experiments should not say much. Their size and shape can be completely arbitrary. Of course, they should not leak water at all and should not in any way affect the properties of the nutrient solution. Therefore, it is not permissible for the walls of the vessels to secrete any substance or absorb anything from the solution.

Building Your Own Hydroponic System

A wide variety of materials from which experimental vessels can be made (metals, plastic, ceramics, porcelain, concrete, etc.). It compels us to give one completely justified advice: each vessel should be covered with an insulating layer in places where its surface comes into contact with the nutrient solution. Double coating with good bitumen paint fully meets the purpose and eliminates unpleasant surprises. However, in this case, you should not confuse bitumen paint with often very similar preparations from coal tar containing substances poisonous to plants.

Earth excavations, wooden troughs, and other tanks can be made waterproof with plastic films. Many amateur and vegetable growers-producers use earthen ditches for growing plants, and these dredges fully justify themselves provided that they were coated with phenol-free films. The fact is that some of the plastic films, in contact with the nutrient solution, release substances poisonous to plants. For this reason, you have to constantly recommend when you buy a film and indicate its intended purpose. In this case, you will be offered the most suitable type of film.

Substrates or Fillers
What requirements should material use as a substrate meet? It must be a substance with the following properties:

- with rather large particles that would not spill out between the battens of the crate or between the mesh cells;

- able to absorb and retain a large amount of water so that it is not required to moisturize it daily with a nutrient solution;
- resistant against decomposition and not able to rot;
- chemically neutral, that is, one that does not emit any products that can damage plants, and in no way affects the nutrient solution.

What materials meet these requirements and which of them can we use?

The cultural substrate in which the plants will take root must be selected very carefully and, if necessary, subjected to preliminary processing. In recent years, suitability for this series of materials has been studied, many of which have been deemed suitable. We will consider only the most important of them, which have already become widespread.

In principle, it can be stated that all used cultural substrates differ in the following qualities:

- they are chemically neutral and, thus, have no effect on the properties and chemical composition of the nutrient solution;
- high resistance to weathering and decomposition allows them to maintain their structure for a long time;
- they are loose, and you can dig into them with your bare hands without fear of injury;
- they are all more or less hygroscopic and, thus, provide capillary lifting of liquids.

We now turn to the description of individual materials that have passed the test in practice. Let's start with the substrate, which is often indicated in the literature as ideal. Since recently it can be purchased in many and most countries, it may be of interest to us as well. Let's see what experts say about "vermiculite".

"Vermiculites" are secondary minerals that have arisen as a result of hydrothermal changes in two types of mica: biotite and phlogopite. These are water-containing magnesium-aluminum silicates, mostly found as inclusions in such highly basic rocks as dunite, serpentine, and pyroxenite, and often, and vice versa, including these rocks. So far, deposits of vermiculite have been discovered in South Africa (Transvaal), Tanganyika, USA (Colorado,

Montana), Western Australia, the USSR (Urals), and Japan.

Now, 17 varieties of vermiculite are already known. The following composition can be indicated as an approximate composition: 5% AL2O3, Fe2O3, 22% SiO2, 40% H2O2. Vermiculite ore is stratified like mica and is colored from dark yellow-brown to light brownish yellow, green or bronze. The specific gravity of the rock is 2.3 - 2.9, and after stratification - 0.9. Hardness 1.5, melting point about 1360 degrees, water content 4 to 20%. Mining is carried out in open pits and to a lesser extent by explosive means. The rock is coarsely ground and dried to facilitate further processing. After this, the rock is milled and sorted by particle size using pneumatic devices. Heating the ore to dry it is permissible only for a short time and not more than 140 degrees.

The value of vermiculite lies in its property to increase in volume when heated by almost 15 times. Heating causes the conversion of chemically bound water into steam, separating microscopic plates that are layered on top of each other. At a temperature of 900-1100 degrees, the ore is brought to a red glow, but this temperature should not be maintained for more than 4-8 seconds. After that, the ore is cooled as quickly. As a result of these two processes, it turns into a granular, extremely light, stable, free-flowing product. This treatment of vermiculite is called delamination. After processing, the final product turns from silver to gold.

The following properties make layered vermiculite valuable and explain the rapid growth of its use, limited only by its insufficient production: low weight (1 cubic meter weighs 100-125 kg), incombustibility, impermeability (only 6.2% moisture after content at 100% relative humidity for 300 hours), indestructibility, indecomposability, resistance to insects and rodents, and above all an insulating effect in relation to heat, cold, sound, and electricity.

Here is the complete chemical composition of South African vermiculite: SiO2 - 39.37; TiO2 - 1.25; Al2O2 - 12.08; Fe2O3 - 5.48; FeO - 1.17; MnO - 0.30; MgO - 23.37; CaO - 1.46; Na2O - 0.80; K2O - 2.46; H2O - 11.09, CO2 - 0.60; P2O5 - 0.15; Li2O - 0.03; BaO - 0.03; Cl - 0.02; SO3 - 0.02; S - 0.18; * at 105C. From this technical description, we can conclude that layered-in vermiculite is an ideal material as a substrate for growing plants without soil: it is chemically inert, free-flowing, absorbs water well, and retains its structure perfectly. According to US practice, it can be used to grow plants without any pre-treatment.

In Europe, coarse-grained pumice and foamy lava are currently preferred. We are talking about igneous rocks, somewhat similar to a sponge, and therefore, have extremely high absorption capacity. Both breeds have a stable structure and loose, but their chemical properties are not ideal. They contain quite a lot of free lime and other compounds, which subsequently very readily enter into undesirable exchange reactions with a nutrient solution. In this case, various important components of the nutrient solution pass into a form in which they can no longer be absorbed by plants.

However, these shortcomings can be eliminated through very simple operations. So, for example, we can wash gravel from the pumice of highly diluted sulfuric acid until the evolution of gas bubbles ceases. After this, the gravel from which the lime has been removed is left for many hours in clean water, after which it is thoroughly washed in running water. At the end of the flushing, such gravel can be used without any concern.

Another method of neutralizing gravel is keeping it for a day in a solution of superphosphate in boiled water (750 g of superphosphate per 10 liters of water). After a day, the excess solution is drained, and the gravel is washed with clean water, which ends its processing.

In many areas, you can easily purchase blast furnace slag, which after special treatment can also be used as a substrate. What is this? It is made from the slag from blast furnaces, a liquid by-product of iron smelting, converted by the action of water vapor into a gravel-like, highly porous material.

Unfortunately, blast furnace slag has even higher alkalinity than pumice or foamy lava (up to 43% CaO). Despite this, it can be prepared in the same way as pumice, but only in this case, you need to be even more careful to completely remove lime from the substrate. The advantage of thermite is its low cost, which compares very favorably with the previously mentioned materials. For the same reasons, special attention should be paid to coal slag, which can be purchased at a very low price.

For the profitability of industrial soilless plants in most cases, the cost of the culture substrate is a significant burden. Therefore, it is quite natural that the search for cheap substitutes for pumice and similar materials began long ago. Suitable slags are substitutes that are found to be complete in all respects. Amateur gardeners are fortunate in that they can benefit from the experience already gained in the production environment.

Suitable for use are well-calcined coal or coke slag; all other types of slag (for example, brown coal slag) are generally unsuitable for this purpose. The required amount of slag is thoroughly cleaned of foreign debris and then mechanically crushed.

With a large demand for production plants in the substrate, stone crushing machines are mostly used for grinding slag, but we will do with a simple tamper and sledgehammer. From the crushed substrate, we need to select fractions with a particle diameter of 0-15 mm, and here, our assistants will be sieves with the corresponding hole diameter. After that, it is checked whether the substrate needs preliminary chemical treatment.

There can be quite a big difference between the two types of slag, especially regarding their suitability for growing plants without soil. Source material, combustion temperature, and other factors play an important role. It is often necessary to pre-treat the slag to remove toxic substances from it, especially sulfur compounds and, of course, lime.

The test is very simple. About 1 liter of the test material is taken from the slag mass and poured into a glass jar for canning. About 0.5 l of water is poured into the second jar of the same and very carefully add an equal amount of concentrated sulfuric acid to this jar (Sulfuric acid is diluted by pouring it into the water, but you can never pour water into acid. This is very dangerous!). This diluted acid is poured into the slag until it is completely coated with the solution. If foam begins to form on the surface of the solution, gas bubbles with the smell of rotten eggs appear, then all the slag must be chemically treated. However, if nothing like this happens, then we are extremely lucky and managed to get a completely usable slag.

The small amounts of slag required for our purposes are best immediately poured into vessels coated with bitumen paint and filled with sulfuric acid diluted in a ratio of 1:10 (10 l of water per 1 l of acid). After waiting when the formation of foam and gas bubbles ceases, a small sample is again taken from the water-washed slag and subjected to the above test with an acid in a glass jar. This is necessary because it is very likely that the first pretreatment of all substrate weights could be insufficient to convert all hazardous compounds into gaseous hydrogen sulfide (with the smell of rotten eggs) or into water-soluble sulfates. Thus, if foam appears again in the glass jar and gas bubbles rise, then the whole procedure should be repeated with a freshly prepared acid solution.

Before the final use of the slag, it is very thoroughly washed with ordinary water to remove all compounds that have been converted into a soluble state as a result of processing, as well as sulfuric acid residues. To verify the completeness of acid removal in drain water (after repeated washing), a litmus paper is lowered (such paper will be needed in the future to check the pH of the nutrient solution); in this case, only a slightly acidic reaction is permissible. After that, the slag is ready for consumption.

We will not hide that slags, in one respect, do not quite meet our requirements: the sharp edges of the particles make the slag somewhat less loose and you have to work with it more carefully. However, this disadvantage can be largely eliminated by adding to the slag (before the treatment just described) about 10% silica sand.

Quartz sand, basalt chips, and crushed granite are chemically neutral due to the high content of silicates in them. Unfortunately, they do not absorb moisture and their particles have very sharp edges (in particular, granite and basalt). They can at best be used as impurities to other materials, such as slag or pumice.

When growing certain crops that prefer moderately moist habitats (such as cacti, etc.), it is very useful to add basalt chips to other water-absorbing substrates.

We refrain from using crumb brick, although it was often recommended in some previous publications. Here, in most cases, you have to reckon with a very high content of lime, which must be removed. In addition, the crumb brick does not have a particularly stable structure. After a very short time, sludge deposits form at the bottom of our earthen excavation or vessel, which is agitated when the nutrient solution is drained and leads to blockage of pipes and other interferences. The nutrient solution itself is colored with silt in a reddish color, which complicates the analysis of the solution, and in some cases simply makes it impossible. Finally, in the brick crumb, very often, there are many extraneous impurities of an indeterminate nature (resins, metals, etc.), which, as substances, that are potentially toxic to plants.

In recent studies, it was possible to prove that the presence of humic substances in the cultural substrate of a plant for growing plants without soil has a direct and beneficial effect on plants. This in no way contradicts our previous reasoning, since humic substances, in this case, do not act as a source of plant nutrition. The action of humic substances is manifested due to the following features.

- They contribute to the absorption of nutrients because they increase the solubility of mineral salts and prevent them from precipitating from solution (the formation of complexes with organic compounds). In addition, it turned out that plant roots coated with a layer of humic substances better absorb inorganic nutrients.

- Due to the presence of humic substances, the nutrient solution acquires "buffering", that is, greater resistance to reaction bias.

- Humus contains various soluble humic substances or related products such as antibiotics, growth substances, estrogen substances, etc., which can be absorbed by the plant and contribute to its better development.

Given these circumstances, it is not difficult to understand why, at present, some organic matter, mostly peat, is willingly mixed into the substrate. A mixture of half volumes of inorganic gravel and peat has proven itself, and in some places, they work successfully with pure peat. In the following, we will return to this issue and trace the development of individual plants in pure gravel, as well as for comparison in a mixture of gravel with peat or in pure peat. In this case, it is necessary to carefully note which particular plant species respond particularly well to the presence of humic substances.

The substrate from a mixture of peat chips and bed peat is well aerated. No matter how wet the substrate is, the roots of the plants still get enough oxygen for respiration, in addition, this mixture does not melt. Peat is difficult to decompose, and even with strong moisture and high temperature, it is unlikely to rot.

Chapter 4: Good Plants for Hydroponic System (Vegetables, Fruits, Flowers and Herbs)

Valerian

Valerian is a herbaceous plant that originates in central Europe and Asia but is now widespread also in western Europe and North America. The valerian develops very broadly and can reach a height of one and a half meters. The rhizome of the valerian plant is composed of many roots that are characterized by an unpleasant smell.

The typical environment of the valerian is the areas rich in humidity, the margins of the courses of the rivers, woods, etc.. However, we can cultivate it very well even in our gardens when it has no particular needs. The optimal climate for the cultivation of valerian is the temperate one, however, this plant can withstand even temperatures of fifteen degrees below zero; likes sun exposure but also semi-shaded.

Valerian is multiplied by seed, by the division of the rhizome or tuft. Before proceeding with sowing, the soil will be worked deeply. If seed multiplication is chosen, it will be done during the spring period starting from the seedbed; this operation takes a long time because the valerian has a very slow development.

Basil

Basil is one of the most cultivated aromatic plants in Italy; in fact, it is a small herbaceous plant, native to Asia, which came to Europe centuries ago, and has been cultivated both in Europe and in Asia for a very long time. In fact, the basil we are used to eating and seeing in the garden is a hybrid plant, whose botanical name is Ocimum Basilicum "Genoese", testimony to the city where the use of basil is more widespread. It is a perennial plant, generally cultivated as an annual, as it fears the cold, and temperatures below 10°C cause its rapid deterioration. Basil, as we know it, is just one of several varieties spread in cultivation; in fact, in the Italian kitchen we particularly appreciate the so-called sweet basil, with a large leaf and a delicate aroma

Borage

Borage alias cucumber. Borage has a taste of fresh green cucumber, which makes it excellent in salads or on spreads. In medicine, the seeds of the plant or the borage oil derived from it are used mainly for skin complaints.

Watercress

Watercress, also called bach or watercress, botanically belongs to the family brassica (Brassicaceae). In addition to the genuine watercress (nasturtium officinale), the small-leaved watercress (nasturtium microphyllum) is very common in Germany. The original range of the two species probably extended over Europe, North Africa, and southwest Asia. Meanwhile, watercress as a neophyte, however, can be found almost worldwide. It likes to settle on shady, clear, shallow waters with a slight current, for example, at sources or in the shallow riparian zones of clean streams. Watercress is a beautiful water plant for gardens: it does not only look pretty, but it is also delicious. Watercress: location, and cultivation.

Watercress is a marsh and aquatic plant and thrives best in water depths of 5 to 20 centimeters. It is, therefore, quite expensive to grow them in gardens.

A natural source of water is best for planting watercress. Which makes it suitable for hydroponics. It often grows in nature at the edge of small streams and moats.

You can grow watercress in the pot by pressing the seeds lightly on the ground and keeping them moist. At a temperature of 20 degrees, the seeds begin to germinate after about a week. If the young plants have reached a height of 8 to 10 centimeters, you can put them at the appropriate watering place.

The true watercress was already in ancient times as a medicinal plant cultured. Due to its high vitamin c content, the plant was especially valued as an anti-scurvy. It is also considered a blood purifier. Its name derives from the Latin name "nasus tortus", a twisted nose in English - an expression that results from the reaction to the consumption of the slightly pungent cress type.

The cultivation of watercress is worthwhile not only because of the beautiful sight, but it is also extremely healthy: watercress is rich in vitamins c, a, k, and b2 and was, therefore, one of the few foods in the winter months against scurvy. In addition, it contains iodine, iron, and calcium, as well as mustard oils. They provide a slightly pungent taste and have an antibacterial and digestive effect.

In natural medicine, the fresh leaves of watercress are recommended as a home remedy for cystitis and congested respiratory tract and to stimulate digestion and kidney activity.

Angelica

The angelica is one of the few medicinal plants that are native to northern Europe and from the north - Greenland and Iceland - by planting in the medieval monastery gardens in the 14th century. Central Europe has become their habitat. For about 500 years, the effects of this magnificent and stately plant in herbal books are described. The spectrum ranges from folk medicine to modern phytotherapy, from the protection against a plague disease to the magenta therapeutic. Its manifold application in the past has brought the angelica also many more names, so we find for them names such as butterbur, theraminwurz, brustwurz, heiliggeistwurz, according to their preferred use. In the alpine region, we often find the wild angelica or waldengelwurz - angelica sylvestris l. Although it also reaches a height of more than one meter and is thus an attractive umbelliferae in the landscape

From these effects, the following fields of application for this aromatic amarum (bitter agent) can be derived: loss of appetite can thus be favorably influenced; if dyspeptic symptoms and mild gastrointestinal spasms are present, these can be well removed with preparations from the root of the angelica. Often, feelings of fullness and bloating are triggered by stressful situations that also respond well to this medicinal plant.

In addition to the medicinal use of the angelica root, it is also processed in herb schnapps, liqueurs, and another digestive (digestive preparations); but also, the seasoning of sauces, salads, and other foods is the tart aroma of angelica. The flower stems of the plant are used for candying and thus form a sweet variation in Austrian pastry art.

Fennel

Fennel is native to the Mediterranean but is now grown worldwide. There are various sub-forms, of which the seeds and the fennel green are used for seasoning or the fennel tuber as vegetables.

Fennel has a sweet, aniseed taste. The leaves and tubers are used, especially in the Mediterranean cuisine for fish and salads. The seeds spice soups, sauces, grilled meat, and fish, but also taste in bread and cake in alcoholic drinks such as pastis or absinthe, fennel rounds off the taste of anise.

Fennel needs warm and sunny locations with light, not too moist soil; it is relatively sensitive. As medicinal plant fennel has many effects: it helps against flatulence and abdominal pain, in diseases of the upper respiratory tract and as an infusion against eye pain and inflamed eyelids.

Cucumbers

Hydroculture for cucumbers with your own hands will be very welcome in the economy if you want to get a good harvest of this vegetable quickly. Cucumbers are climbers, so it is better in small hydroponics to sow them along the wall of the pallet, and after the shoots appear, bind them to the installed at an angle stops. This method helps breeders looking for a way to grow cucumbers quickly. Such placement of cucumbers does not disturb other plants that may also be in this range, and the bound cucumbers eventually produce fruits of much higher quality. Optimal growth of cucumbers contributes to the bright day up to 14 hours.

Varieties of cucumbers for growing in hydroponics

The most popular cucumbers for hydroponic cultivation are "European" or "long English" cucumbers. Beit alpha (ba), Japanese or Persian varieties are becoming increasingly popular (photo 2). They are similar to the European cucumbers but are smaller (usually 10-15 cm) and in contrast to the European cucumbers with an average size of 30 to 35 cm. These cucumbers are gutted and have thin skin and do not need to be cleaned when preparing salads. Due to its thin skin, the necessary moisture in the room must be maintained to avoid weight loss. European species - occupy the second place for hydroponic crops with high yields in confined spaces. Unlike tomato plantations, which are more robust, cucumber is more tender. They must be constantly kept under special growth conditions in order to achieve maximum yields. When cucumbers are left unattended, they quickly get entangled, and yields drop dramatically. They are then almost impossible to untangle, unlike tomatoes. Therefore, proper care is required throughout the growth cycle.

What you need to grow cucumbers in hydroponics

If you want to grow tomatoes and cucumbers in your own cottage, you will need to purchase a hydroponic installation. If the purchase is not possible, you can create it yourself. This requires:

- Expanded clay
  - Plastic pipes for further planting
  - Pump
  - Mineral wool
  - Mineral fertilizers
  - Compost layer
  - Selected medium gravel
  - Capacity for plants, mostly glasses
- Water

The technology of growing cucumbers with hydroponics
Hydroponics will help to cultivate cucumbers in the home, comparable to those grown in the garden. It is necessary to follow the technology of cultivation strictly.

Sowing seeds in cassettes
First, the cork stoppers are soaked in a nutrient solution; then, a cucumber core is placed in the centre of each cork. Hydroponics contains many nutrients in the solution that help to saturate the seed from within. Powder vermiculite will help to create an optimal humid environment. After planting, the seeds of the cassette are covered with a plastic wrap, which is removed after 3 days. The temperature to be followed is 23-25 ° c.

Replanting sprouts into cubes
Cubes, such as cassettes, are subjected to a solution treatment (as described in the article) to prepare a hydroponic solution, after which seven days of shoots can be transferred there. You should take a seedling with a cork and transfer it to a cube to reduce the temperature by 1 degree. The increased distance between the cubes contributes to the normal development of the plants. Sprouting seedlings in such conditions are 1.5 months.

Transplanting cucumber seedlings in mats
Before you plant cucumbers at home, the mats must be soaked in a solution. Make small holes in the packaging that serve as a drainage function. It should take place at a temperature of +22-25°C. After the beginning of flowering, the seedling forms a stem, after which the fifth leaf must remove all flowers.

The germination of the roots in the mat should be done at a temperature of +21-22 °C.

Features care for cucumbers
If we have decided to grow cucumbers at home, we have to take good care of them. Before the formation of the first fruit, the stalk must be constantly removed. As the number of cucumbers increases, it is worthwhile to control the transition from vegetative to generative growth. Cucumbers should be carefully watered, with sprinkling begun 2 hours after sunrise and 2 hours before sunset to avoid deformation of the fruit. The temperature should not exceed + 19-22°C and + 24°C on sunny days. It is necessary to ventilate the greenhouse regularly, maintaining a humidity of 70-80% to avoid mildew and botrytis.

Advantages and disadvantages of growing cucumbers with hydroponics
The advantages of hydroponics are:

- The fast growth of cucumbers
    - Fruit does not accumulate harmful chemicals, which has a positive effect on human health.
    - Space-saving in a similar type of cultivation,
    - If necessary, plants can be transplanted to another location,
    - One of the main advantages of the method is that no land is needed, which is particularly important in areas with a lack of fertile land.
- Cucumbers do not need to be poured frequently.

There are virtually no disadvantages to this type of cultivation, but there are negative features:

- Spending on equipment
- Performing frequent monitoring of the temperature regime of plants.

Tomatoes

Hydroponic seedlings, including tomatoes, are grown in small pots floating or suspended over water so that the tomato roots absorb the necessary amount of nutrient-rich water necessary for the tomatoes or other hydroponic plants to grow. An unsinkable support system must first be built or purchased in order to plant and grow using the hydroponic method.

Instructions

Purchase hydroponic plant trays for growing tomatoes. Trays with larger holes are used to better support adult tomato plants (remember, if you want to grow the tomatoes completely in the hydroponic beds or pimp them in a garden or pot during the warm growing season).

Use a cutter to cut larger holes in hydroponic plant trays with holes for adult tomato plants too small. Be careful not to let the lower ends taper conically to allow the root system to fall through to provide better watering results.

Purchase or build a waterbed to place the trays. Build the beds of wooden frames on the inside covered with a single solid sheet or plastic.

Fill the plant tray holes halfway down the ground and drop a tomato seed into each hole. Cover the seeds, fill the tray with holes, and then place in the waterbeds, where the trays remain over water at the surface of the water, with only enough of the tray so that the tomato plant roots can absorb the necessary amount of water.

Tips and warnings

Monitor the growth of the plants. Of course, as the plants grow, they will become heavier; if the plants are too heavy to be supported by the trays, you will need to use other materials to support the trays. You do not want to soil the trays by more than an inch deep and risk drowning the root system of the tomatoes. Bricks work to support the shells and prevent them from sinking too deep into the water.

Chapter 5: Maintenance of a Hydroponic System

Hydroponic gardens need to have proper care and maintenance, or they will not produce healthy plants. Not only do they need to be constantly cleaned, but there are various maintenance checks that need to be carried out in order to make sure the system remains functioning correctly.

A faulty drain or a leaky pipe or switch could do serious damage to a hydroponic garden as most of the systems rely on their equipment and parts to work smoothly.

Cleanliness

In order to stop the build-up of algae, mold, and fungus or to stop attracting pests, keep the growing room as clean as possible.

Equipment should be flushed and cleaned at least twice a month to maintain water levels, stop algae growth, and ensure that there are no pests lurking about the system.

In order to stop pests and various fungal growth, growers should always make sure their hands are clean. Hands should be kept washed especially after handling anything that was dirty or in contact with a harmful substance.

Do not let old fallen leaves, stems, fruit, produce or growing media or even pots or discarded trays lie around the growing areas. Rather throw out any debris or broken items, and wash and pack away any unused equipment.

Wash all equipment after use and only reuse a growing medium if it can be reused and it has been thoroughly washed and sterilized. In fact, all growing mediums, whether old or new, should be thoroughly washed before being used as not to contaminate the grow pots, grow trays, and the reservoir.

Keeping the growing area and equipment clean cuts down on the chances of infestation and development of frustrating diseases that are a nuisance to get rid of.

Nutrient Solution

The proper nutrient solution for the plant type and system type should be used at the correct ratio of solution to water.

Only use good quality nutrient solutions with an organic base. Advance nutrients are only required should there be a problem that needs to be fixed, such as a nutrient deficiency in a plant.

The nutrient solution balance should be checked on a regular basis especially is it is a recovery system where the solution is being continuously recycled.

Make sure that the solution is flushed and completely refreshed on a regular basis and that there is no salt buildup since this is very acidic and toxic to the plants.

Watering

Watering is done in many different ways and is delivered to each of the hydroponic systems differently.

Make sure the water is always fresh and checked on a regular basis. Algae is a common problem, as is nutrient build up in the system. An oxygen pump should be installed in order to ensure the water is being well hydrated and to keep the water fresher for longer.

Water solutions can come from the tap, drain systems, or rain collection tanks.

Watering can be on a continuous flow basis or set by a timer that switches on and off at different intervals during the day.

If possible, a person should always have a backup water solution available in case of an emergency and their primary watering source is unavailable. Some plants are very sensitive to their watering schedule and even a few minute's downtimes and a missed watering schedule can cause some damage.

Reservoir Temperature

The water in the reservoir should be around 65 to 75 degrees Fahrenheit, which is the basic room temperature. Water that is either too hot or too cold can damage the plant's root systems and their leaves.

The reservoir should be topped off with water in order to keep pH and nutrient levels constant. Change out the water on a regular basis.

Humidity

Different plants and hydroponic systems need the humidity to be on different levels. There are thermometers that can measure the humidity and temperature to ensure that the plants are comfortable. Keeping an optimum level does not encourage the growth of unwanted diseases and fungi.

Make sure plants that love the hotter temperatures get enough humidity by giving them a regular misting spray. This will help to keep the humidity constant for the plants that do not like too much humidity.

Inspect the Equipment

The equipment should be thoroughly inspected on a regular basis.

There are a lot of things that can go wrong in a hydroponic system, especially with the equipment. And the best way to troubleshoot is to try to avoid as many equipment malfunctions as possible.

The best way to inspect equipment is to keep the entire system in mind. When doing the inspection starts at one point and work your way through your system.

Start with the reservoir and all the systems that are dependent on it.

- Water feeding pipe

    o   This should be thoroughly checked for crimps that may not be feeding the solution correctly.
    o   Nutrients build up in the pipes so they may need thorough flushing out or replacing.
    o   Check for any blockages in the pipe.
    o   Check for any holes or leaks that could deter the flow of water pressure in the pipe.
    o   Check for any algae or mold that may be growing in or around the pipe.
    o   Determine if it may be time to replace the hoses.
    o   Give them a good cleaning if they are still viable.

- Nozzles and hoses

    o   Check the nozzles that feed the root systems, sprinklers, or misting systems.
    o   When last were they changed?
    o   Check for blockages or leakage.
    o   Check any joins and washers for leaks.
    o   Check for sediment build-up, algae, or mold growing in or around these attachments.

- o   Give them a good cleaning if they are still usable.
- Drain siphons and hoses

    - o   Check the drain pipes for blockages
    - o   When last were they replaced?
    - o   Check for leaks.
    - o   Check for algae or mold growing in or around these pipes.
    - o   They may need to have a good cleaning as part of the system maintenance.

- Check the reservoir water pump

    - o   Test the pump
    - o   Make sure it is still working correctly and pumping the water at the optimum flow.
    - o   Check that all pump attachments are not leaking air.

- Check the reservoir

    - o   Check that there is no build-up, algae, or mold growing on the reservoir.
    - o   Check for any leaks.
    - o   Make sure the water is at the optimum temperature for the hydroponic system and plants.
    - o   Check that any air pumps are functioning correctly and adequately oxygenating the tank.
    - o   Make sure any oxygen stones do not have unwanted algae or mold growth on them

- Growing trays

    - o   Make sure the growing tray(s) do not have any leaks in them.
    - o   Make sure the growing tray(s) are clean and have not unwanted algae or mold growing on them.
    - o   Clean off any nutrient build-up and make sure the trays are clean.
    - o   For a closed system, the trays must be given thorough flushing out.

- Growing pots

    - o   Check that each of the pots is still intact and not broken.
    - o   Replace any that are not functioning correctly.
    - o   Make sure any growing medium is clean and does not have any unwanted algae or mold growing on them that could upset the plant's

natural balance.

- Lighting equipment

  - o Check that the bulbs are still functioning correctly.
  - o Check that the lighting is still adequate for the environment.
  - o Check the timers are working correctly.
  - o Clean any residue off the lighting system.

  Temperature

  - o Make sure that any thermostat is working correctly, and that room temperature is normal.
  - o Check that the humidity is correct for the growing environment.
  - o Check both the temperature and humidity thermometers to ensure that they are still working correctly.

  Ventilation

  - o Make sure that there is adequate ventilation in the growing room.
  - o Not enough ventilation can cause mold.
  - o Check that all fans and cooling systems are working correctly.

- Support Systems

  - o Check that any hanging supports for the plants are working without causing the plant or system any undue stress.
  - o Make sure that the environment in which the hydroponic system is housed offers the correct infrastructure for the system to function correctly.
  - o Make sure the plants are all supported and planted correctly to ensure a successful infrastructure.

  Tools

  - o Are all the gardening tools in working order?
  - o Are they cleaned?
  - o Are there any that may need to be replaced?

Look at Your Plants

Make sure you keep a vigilant check on your growing plants. Measure their growth rate, root growth and when they are ready to harvest.

This gives a person a good measure of how the next batch should perform and something by which to determine if the growing medium, solution, or systems structure may need to be changed or optimized.

The plants must also be checked to make sure they are getting enough nutrients, they are growing as they should, and there are no pests or other infestations. A lot of growing problems and deficiencies can be caused by various infestations. Some are easy to spot, others may take more of an experienced eye, but as a gardener gets to know their plants they will come to instinctively know when something is wrong.

Look for the signs in seedlings such as slow growth, looking sad and droopy, white fluffy stuff growing on the leaves, etc.

Take the time to look over the plants; do not just rush through it. If there are a lot of plants to look over, break them into sections and do a revolving sweep of one section on this day, and the next section on another.

If there is an outbreak, you will need to go through the entire growing area right away.

Spending time with the plants in a hydroponic environment can also be quite good for the mind and spirit. Plants and running water are rather therapeutic and can reduce stress, anxiety and ease tension.

Change One Thing at a Time

If you are wanting to change or expand your system, do not try and do it all at once.

Choose a section to change, switch it around, or upgrade and start with that.

Before rushing out and buying expensive parts, why not try a bit of DIY and try to make it yourself. Or at least look around to see what you have available before rushing off to spend more money on an item you do not really need.

Hydroponic systems are not only flexible and versatile in what they can grow or how they deliver their solutions, but they can also be easily adapted to suit the grower's needs and lifestyle.

There are so many great DIY ideas on how to create the perfect hydroponic garden online these days that it is well worth a try. The money you save building the system yourself can be better spent on plants, growing media, or nutrient solutions.

In order to keep a system simple and working for you, think carefully about an upgrade or addition. Plot it out and then work through one section at a time getting that part right before moving on to the next.

Chapter 6: Pest Prevention and Troubleshooting

Nutrition for hydroponics:

There are some basics of the hydroponic system, and nutrients are one of them. This section will help you understand all you need to know about applying and giving your crops the right nutrients for its survival in the system.

Since you need to meet all your plant needs, then you will have to know what you are supplying to the plant and what can be wrong if you do it too much or do not do it at all. Just as with any nutrient media, there are two things that you need to keep in your mind just as you are about to begin your hydroponic; the composition of the nutrient and the fact about all the nutrients that are supposed to contain. Secondly, you have to know what strength of this nutrient is needed for the particular crop that you are planting. This is very important as the survival of your crop is based on your understanding of this.

Composition of the nutrient solution

Several persons who grow the hydroponic system would want to buy a premixed media or nutrient solution, and this even needs to be diluted in water before use. Some of these already made nutrients usually come in 2,3 or even more parts, this is so that the grower can diversify the ratio of the mineral elements, and this can allow for a very productive vegetative growth for all the crops.

There are good brands of the already made nutrients in the market, but then you can easily have some challenges when you want to use them; this is because they have already been prepared for plants that would grow on soil hence have to be taken when you want to feed them to your plant in the hydroponic system.

However, there is a nutrient mix that is hydroponic specific, and you should get these; for the nutrient mix to be seen as complete, then they have to contain these elements. Nitrogen, phosphorus, potassium, calcium, sulfur, magnesium, manganese, copper, Iron, Boron Chlorine, Molybdate.

The concentration of these elements in your nutrient mix and then the right concentration that is best for your plant depends on the brand of the product of the nutrient mix you purchase. This is so because there is no specific recommendation for the concentrations. Some brands may also contain elements like Cobalt, Silica, Nickel, or selenium. While these are not so essential, plants can grow very well without them, yet they are quite needed for the optimum growth of many crops.

Problems with nutrients:

Whether you choose to make your nutrient solution from the different fertilizer salt or you buy an already made nutrient mix, you are also prone to encountering problems, and this usually appears as the deficiency; that is, the plant can come up with the deficiency of several nutrients. A good reason for this is a case where the nutrient is too low than the required needed concentration; the formula you are using not being balanced; some other times, growers may skip a particular nutrient salt or altogether use a wrong fertilizer when trying to weigh out the nutrient formula.

Also, even when all the factors are set right, the plant can have some internal issues that would prevent it from taking up nutrients; this can lead to deficiency and symptoms that can result.

Signs of Deficiency:

Several signs will detect deficiency when the necessary nutrients are lacking in the plants. These symptoms are quickly traced to the nutrients that are being required, and then they are supplied quickly. The growers will need to know these signs for easy detection.

A lot of these signs are quite easily detected, and they can be also similar to the other deficiency. Some of them, however, are quite distinct, but then since we are giving you quite something to worth your while, it is okay that you get the very symptoms of these, so you can easily.

Below is a list of the symptoms of deficiency for the elements that are needed by the hydroponic system for each of the elements; you should, however, note that these symptoms may be different for some crops, but this list should guide you to have an idea of what exactly the problem is.

Nitrogen

Plants that are deficient in this element are usually very short, the leaves are very pale looking and have some yellow spot colors on them. However, in the tomato crop, the leaves and the steps do not show yellow. Instead, they have a purple coloration underneath the leaves and on the stems.

Phosphorus

Plants deficient in phosphorus have a dark green color, and also appear to be stunted; this symptom is first seen in the older leaves before the newer leaves. Also, there is a delay in the maturity of the plant. The weather can affect the uptake of nutrients by plants, and sometimes, the cold weather can be the reason why a plant show phosphorus deficiency and not necessarily because there is a lack.

Potassium

For this element, a deficiency is suspected when the old leaves will become yellow, and then they are dark spots that are scattered around the leaves; the death of the plant soon follows this. When there is a severe deficiency, it will lead to stunted; all the leaves will be yellowed and curled. The lettuce crop will tend to appear bronze, and also this begins from the matured foliage.

Sulfur

This element is usually available, and the deficiency is not very common; there can be yellowing of leaves, and this can be seen in small and new plants grow.

Magnesium; this is quite common for the tomato crop when it does occur, there can be yellowing of leaves, and this happens between the vein and which remains green.

Calcium

Deficiency in calcium affects the older leaves, and they become distorted; they are small in size because they have spotted and dead areas of the plant. This deficiency inhibits the development of bud, and the root tips will sometimes die back. When the tip burn occurs on the lettuce plant is a case of Calcium deficiency. When the root of the tomato crop blossoms, then it is a calcium deficiency, and this is seen as a deficiency in the fruit and not in the nutrient solution. And this is a transport problem within the plant; the plant has issues with transporting calcium from the nutrient media to its fruits. Several environmental factors can cause this problem.

Iron

This deficiency is quite distinct, it is seen as the yellowing of leaves while the veins remain green; this is first observed on the new leaves and growth. It differentiates it from magnesium deficiency, which begins its yellowing from older leaves. On other crops like tomatoes, iron deficiency can be because of the cold weather and not caused because of the actual lack of nutrient media.

Chlorine

This deficiency is seen as wilted leaves, and then the leaves become yellowed, they turn to bronze color and then become necrotic. The roots of plants that have chlorine deficiency will become stunted and have thick near their tips.

Manganese

There is a beginning yellowing at the intervener leaves of the older leaves, and this depends on the plant types. The leaves get dried and brown areas, and then they begin to drop.

Boron

When plants suffer from a deficiency in boron, the size of the plant begins to reduce; the plant, as it is growing, begins to die; there is a little bit of swelling that is noticed in the root system. The leaves are then thickened, they are yellow with some spots, and then they also appeared curled.

Zinc

A deficiency in zinc will result in stunted growth of the plants and a corresponding reduction in the internode and the size of the leave. The edges of the leave may become distorted and puckered; there can also be yellow spots between the veins.

Copper

It is quite hard to get a deficiency of this element. However, young leaves will have dark green colors, and they will become twisted, with dry and brown spots

Molybdenum

This affects the older leaves majorly because they will have yellowing between their veins; it then moves to the younger leaves; the edges of the leaves will then develop cupping of leaves.

The solution to the deficiency:

Once the nutrient you use is complete and balanced, you should know that the concentration will have a primary effect on the development of the crops and plants. This is why it is essential to measure the nutrient solution using a vital unit to measure. Several growers will want to have ppm, while they still use the TDS meter, but there is an improved way of measurement, and that is the EC (electrical conductivity); this is of better accuracy and right way to measure your nutrients.

What the TDS or the PPM does is that it measures the EC of the solution, then they use the approximate conversion to put this to the PPM. The problem with this is that this kind of measurement cannot be accurate; this is because different nutrient elements will usually have varying PPM values. Hence when you use just one PPM value, you will not be able to get the accurate values of each component. The fact remains that, plants usually respond to the EC or the osmotic concentration, hence it is wiser to measure that instead of the PPM. There are lots of EC meters that are sometimes sold as CF meters; they come with the water-resistant pen meter types, and these are popularly used among growers.

Depending on your location, it is quite easy to read the measurements and then also convert from one unit to the other. The standard units used are the Microsiemens or the conductivity factor. There are also units referred to as the Millimhos, millisiemens, and the micromhos.

Here is the conversion between these;

1 millisiemen = 1 millimhos = 1000 microsiemens = 1000 millimhos = 10 CF

When you run the correct EC for a crop, you should be sure to get the right value. This is very important. Several crops such as lettuce and several other green plants will prefer a much lower EC than those of the fruiting crops such as tomatoes. Every crop has its unique EC that will aid its growth.

When a high EC is run for a plant, it's symptoms will be seen as a deficiency. A crop that is exposed to a high EC is likely to be put under stress. There is much water stress, and then the plant begins to lose water, the water in the plant begins to go back into the nutrient media. If the EC is not very severe, you may eventually see growth, which will be quite slower than the duration that was envisaged. But if the plant begins to wilt and dry up, then it means that the EC is entirely too high for the crop.

When the EC is quite lower than it supposed, then the plant will begin to take lots of water, and this can affect the greenness of the plant; the leaves become fluffy and soft and light green.

The fruit will have reduced flavor, and the quality of the harvest will be dry, and the shelf life will also be affected. Other factors affect the EC, and this includes water uptake from the solution and then making the nutrients higher during warm periods; however, the EC must be monitored and regulated frequently.

When you focus on some essential factors, which are the nutrient balance and nutrient concentration, there will be maximum growth and increased yields; as soon as things begin to go wrong, there is a need for you to identify and begin to correct them before it leads to any loss of crop. Ensure that you watch how your crops are doing so you can think of the best line of defense when you notice any deficiency.

Pest prevention:

Products used to control pest infestation in Hydroponics are important but it could be risky applying pest control products when dealing with Hydroponics. Spray damages on plants grown indoors are far more rampant than we can acknowledge, mostly because we attribute these things to something else most times, without realizing that spray bottles can cause our plants harm. What then is the best way to control pests in Hydroponics? Troubleshooting in the safest possible to get rid of the pest problem in Hydroponics. Although these troubleshooting methods might seem a bit scary, owing to its newness, it is regarded by researchers as the most favorable way to get rid of the pest problem for plants grown indoors.

Troubleshooting:

- Using predator bug to feed on pest

- The use of sticky traps

- Use of pyrethrin to destroy spider mite

Chapter 7: Hydroponics as Business

It is indeed a fulfilling moment to harvest crops from your Hydroponic Gardens. Commercial hydroponics is not just about the hydroponic facilities being set up and managed. To be successful and perform a viable operation, you need to learn to do a number of other things:

- Choose the right crops to grow.

- Have a feasible physical layout.

- Handle your staff and finances properly.

- Market your products correctly.

Deciding what plants to grow

When deciding which plants to grow on a business hydroponics farm, consider the following:

- Facility for transplant propagation/cost. What will be the price (in time or money) to get your initial crops?

- How quick are the plants to reproduce if you intend to propagate themselves? Are the crops readily available? Is the proposed planting date the same as the year you expect to begin your operation?

- How easy is it to grow these plants? Do you have the skills to expand these varieties, or do your staff? Unless you have better than average expertise, challenging plants may be more expensive to produce, and more dangerous to get a benefit from.

- How long will it take for the plant to grow? Many plants produce a harvest that is ready for sale within months, and others take years.

- Adequate to your services. Do you have the proper buildings, equipment, and other facilities under consideration to grow the particular plants? Do you have space and money to provide those facilities?

- Climate suitability. What plants are best suited for growing in your climate?

- The environment. Operating with the atmosphere is always more effective than trying to recreate different environments

- Other competent growers are already growing the crop you'd instead grow? Could you bring in a fair market share?

- Distance from potential customers

- Transportation is expensive and can be hazardous. What are the other options available?

- Are the benefits (other than wages) likely to be a fair or sufficient return on your expenditure in terms of time and money

- Your staff skills. Don't pretend to do what you're incompetent to do. It's likely someone with better skills will do it better and cheaper.

Running the trial- records and reporting

Some measurements can give valuable data, including solution analysis, foliar mineral analysis, plant height, leaf area, and leaf area index (LAI), fruit quality assessment, plant dry weight versus fresh weight, water uptake, root dry weight, yields, marketable yields, taste quality assessment, shelf life, and photographs. There may be several features the grower wants to test.

Evaluating the trial

Comparing the test plot against a cure or a set of treatment plots will assess the crop experiment. The trial assessment usually depends on statistical analysis that decides whether observable variations in control and trial plots are likely due to actual differences or incidence by chance. Plant and plots duplication is widely used to enhance statistical estimation. The higher the replication level, the lower the trial error margin.

Generic statistical analysis should be used for analyzing the trial to determine the actual outcome of the trial. It can be confusing to simply look at the species, and draw a conclusion from them. Quantifying the trial by counting plants and doing a comparative analysis of the data is much more useful in determining whether any observed effects are significant. For this to happen, the grower may need to hire a statistician or horticultural consultant's services.

Standards

Like any business, a hydroponic farm must set and adhere to specific requirements if it is to be running lucratively. Those standards can be classified into three major groups:

1. Expenses for efficiency standards
2. Quality standards
3. Quantity standards

Expenses for efficiency standards

A stable relationship must be formed between production cost and selling price. Both of these numerical statistics need to be constantly monitored and held at an acceptable level in order to ensure market productivity. If production costs get too high, income will diminish. In such a case, the selling price must be raised, or the income percentage may become a negative-sum (i.e., you may lose money instead of earning it).

Cost of production

The following factors influence the cost of production:

- Site's costs (rent / lease)

- Cost of sites' facilities (power, natural gas, water, insurance, fees, etc.)

- Costs of products (soil, fertilizer, etc.)

- Unsold product's costs -certain amounts may be destroyed, die, or become invaluable. (Some horticultural companies spend as much as 30 percent of their stock.)

- Expenses on labor (your time, as well as your staff, should be included

- Promotion of marketing (printing, magazines advertising, etc.)

- Selling value (transport, invoicing, etc.)

- Tax (do not forget payroll tax, income tax, etc.)

Profit

This figure must be above and beyond the money you earn as wages. You would better put your money into some form of investment and work for someone else if you only work for wages (without profit). Profit should be higher than the rate you can get if you invest your money elsewhere. Typically, the income should be at least 15-20%. The profit margin in horticultural companies can vary greatly from crop to crop and year to year. You will note that some years, and other years, the income will be meager (perhaps nothing).

The income must be seen over several years on average. New operations should always have enough resources to support them if they have a few bad seasons before good seasons.

Price of Sales
The amount for which the products are sold will vary significantly. This can be because of factors such as overall economic circumstances, general market supply, and consumer demand.

Quality Standards
The following factors are to be taken note of when considering produce quality:

- The general appearance of vitality or health such as marking or lack of markings (e.g., disease, red, bruising, etc.)

- How it tastes or smell (e.g., how sweet or bitter)

- Freshness (i.e., the faster you can sell it after harvest, the better the quality will be).

Quantity Standards
Agricultural processing needs to meet such requirements in terms of the amount, weight, and size of each unit of the commodity being harvested (for instance, how many strawberries you select per square meter annually and how heavy each strawberry will be).

- Size is not critical for some plants, but the number is (for example, orchids are sold as flowers. A little smaller, or larger flower does not make a big difference in cost).

- Weight is important for other crops, but the size does not matter (for example, the beans are sold in kilograms regardless of whether they are small or large).

- Size and weight of other plants are important also (e.g., kilograms of strawberries are sold, but large plants are priced differently than small plants).

Marketing Your Product

Marketing involves everything involved in bringing the product to the end customer. If you want to sell your goods well, all aspects of the process must be identified, and each step must be performed as well as possible. Typical marketing moves are:

- Packaging and handling of the product–this impacts its quality and durability for a potential buyer.

- Transit of the goods.

- Promotion of products.

Considering Your Markets

In general, hydroponic goods, whether they are fruit, vegetables or flowers, are marketed through the following:

1. Direct selling to the public (for example, from your property's packing shed or a stand along the road). Several farmers have boosted their sales with tourism markets and catering for people visiting their land in other ways. In view of the establishing of hydroponic tours along with direct sales of products and perhaps a shop that sells souvenirs, refreshments, etc. It may be viable. Some of those activities can include' choosing your own' purchases, where the public pays a negotiated price for what they buy.
2. Sales through major markets Major cities thrive markets for fruit, vegetables, and flowers where farmers sell their products to business owners. You can hire a booth or sell on these markets via an agent (who usually takes a commission).
3. Direct selling to retail outlets It may be possible for you to

market your products and if you are large enough to make it worthwhile. However, the distribution can be costly and time-consuming and should not be dealt with lightly. Many businesses project goods are produced in factories for manufacturing. Generally, the price paid for the commodity is fixed, restricting yet assured sales the amount of profit the grower can make.

Market Research

One key to success in any company is ' knowing the industry. ' When you know, there is a desire for what you are going to grow, and if you can decide where that market is, the chance of success will greatly increase (not to mention sleepless nights). So one of the many crucial things you can do is research the market in-depth before any new crop is developed. Successful marketing depends on knowing the people/groups you sell–what they want, how they can respond to your goods, and what they are going to spend money on, etc.

If you understand the market place you should take the following steps to successful marketing:

- Set realistic marketing targets.

- Have strategies for achieving those goals

- Evaluate marketing initiative outcomes and change the strategies accordingly.

- Market research includes all the practices that enable managers to make marketing decisions. It tries to make the secret known, and in most instances, it succeeds partially.

Market Research Steps

- What information is required? If a problem exists, interpret it.

- How can I increase sales by 10 percent, for example? Or should I change my way of distributing my products?

- Conduct an inquiry. Review past records related to the problem, talk to people who know who can contribute to this problem. Try to find some relevant information released (for example, in trade magazines, statistical departments, etc.). - You can choose to monitor customers (or potential customers) if more information is required. Note: this entails far more prices.

- If the problem remains beyond you, a professional market research firm may be employed to manage the problem.

Chapter 8: Hydroponic Tips and Tricks for Beginners

Gardening is a field that has developed gradually since the start of time. Since the early days until now, people have tried to develop better techniques to deliver a more effective and easy gardening technique. Different forms and new and better strategies have evolved over the years. Another such method is hydroponics.

Hydroponics helps you to cultivate your plants without any natural hazards throughout the year. Conventional gardening techniques require a number of external factors uncontrollable for plant cultivation.

Incontrollable variables such as different seasons, weather etc. play a key role in yield. Nevertheless, approaches that use water solution instead of soil minimize the risk associated with these variables.

These hydroponic systems can be made in your own home if you are an experienced plant gardener. You can also go online for the kits made available by the company. Such kits are available in different sizes and can be chosen according to your particular needs.

Such kits include the necessary equipment and elements such as lamps, pumps, containers, nutrient systems, etc. In any case, you will need an in-depth understanding of plants and their different aspects.

There are many different aspects that make the Hydroponics device cycle a success. Lighting is such an important aspect. It is necessary that you give the plants sufficient light to grow.

At least a good eight hours of sunlight should be given to young plants for efficient growth. Remember always that too much is bad. Make sure that light is not too high, especially when using multiple lights.

Other very important factors in hydroponics are humidity and temperature. Each living organism has an ideal level of different environmental conditions, such as humidity, temperature, etc. If plants are grown indoors, it is very important for plants to survive in a good environment.

More carbon dioxide can also be introduced into the plant for better growth.

In addition to external conditions, nutrition is equally important. You will be able to better understand their nutritional needs by studying the plants you want to produce.

When you have the necessary nutrient solution in Hydroponics, you must focus on the absorption rate. This ensures that the plant can absorb nutrients without any problems to the best of its ability. The aim of a controlled environment is to be able to change every factor in growing plants to maximize their efficiency.

Air pumps and sleeves can help to improve air circulation throughout the solution. For a fact, the water used in the process can also be used over and over again. Whilst it's best to practice gardening before using the hydroponics, beginners can also grow their favorite plants and vegetables in a smaller size.

Hydroponic gardening is nothing other than soil-free planting. It is an economical way to supply plants with food and water. The soil's purpose is to provide plants with nutrients and to protect the roots of plants.

A plant uses food and water in the soil. The plant is supplied with a full nutrient solution and a growing medium in the hydroponic gardening to sustain the root plants.

It allows plants to access water and food more quickly. If you start your first hydroponic garden, a lot of resources and information can be found online. A good way to begin a hydroponic garden is to obey useful factors during gardening.

Some of them are listed below: Grow: you can grow hydroponically vegetables, flowers and medicinal plants. Many of them include tomatoes, peppers, cucumbers, orchids and medicinal plants. You can start a garden by buying seeds online or just buy it from garden centres.

System or method: There are six types of hydroponic systems that you can use for your greenhouse, including Ebb and Flow, Drip, Aeroponic, N.F.T and Wick System. Any device, lighting, and growing medium that suits your plants, garden size and budget can be selected.

Garden area: whether you need a small or large hydroponic garden, you have to decide. The flow of air and the ability to control moisture and temperature in the room depending on your area of cultivation.

Your garden always needs clean water and safe electricity. A continuous water supply with a good pH level is very critical. You need the electric power supply for indoor gardening to operate water pumps, grow systems and fans.

Accessories: Depending on the complexity and size of your hydroponic garden, various accessories including light timers, fans, water pumps and meters for temperature and humidity measurement are required. Many hydroponic gardeners will help you to pick different garden needs.

Lighting system: Light is the key component if you plan to start an indoor garden. Understand your growing space and choose the perfect lighting for your garden. You can choose high intensity growing lights that provide sunshine to your indoor garden.

Nutrients: You don't use soil in hydroponic gardening to grow plants. You must, therefore, provide the plants with full balanced nutrition. Plants require six types of micronutrients, Nitrogen, Phosphorus, Potassium, Calcium, Sulfur, Magnesium, in particular.

A plant needs some small traces of vitamins, iron, boron, zinc, manganese, cobalt and copper. Choose a perfect solution to provide sufficient macro and micronutrients for your plants.

Growing medium: hydroponic means soilless gardening and therefore soil needs to be replaced by a perfect medium of production. This rising medium provides the plants with nutrients. There are enormous varieties of growing medium that cocoa, organic soil, mats, crushed stones and rock wool can be used.

Hydroponics is not a difficult planting strategy. In this process, the plant nutrients are liquefied during the water. A rising medium substitutes the soil for oxygen, water and nutrients to the roots.

The first step in hydroponics is to buy your supplies. The seeds can be put in rock wool starter cubes that fit well into the typical nursery tray. The rock wool should be soaked overnight in a conditioning solution.

Place a seed in each cube.

In each cube. Place the tile under a fluorescent lamp with a semi-circular rim. Wait for the germination of the seeds and for the roots to come out of the cube base. This is the moment when the roots are transplanted into the hydroponic system.

A large yellow pail is required to serve as the external storage that contains the food and water for your plant. The plant actually sits in a small green pail with small pants. More products include the fluorescent light bulb, root help marbles and plant food.

Punch small holes in the smallholder to prevent too much water from flooding the roots.

Wash the ground from the roots until you see the root system's main part. Handle the roots with great care.

Place some marbles at the bottom of the little bowl. This can be from 1/2 inch to 1 inch to provide enough water and air for proper growth.

Enable the roots to settle at the base to access more water. Fill the bowl with more marbles once this is finished. Inside the larger container, position the small pot until it gets balanced.

You can illuminate the plant to speed up production. Water and feed the plant-based on hydroponic gardening standards. Nutrient, salt and water measure. You need one Miracle Grow tablespoon, another salt tablespoon and one gallon of water.

Combine the solution and pour tenderly on the root until the waterline is almost one inch above the bottom of the small pot in the large container.

Make it a point for your plant to maintain. If the plant leaves turn into another color, a problem can occur. The water should also not be too low or too high. The PH balance is better known. To address this problem, change the water regularly. In any hydroponic supply store, PH level test tools can be purchased.

GREENHOUSE GARDENING

*Improve Your System
with A Greenhouse Building
to Grow Better Vegetables, Fruits,
Flowers and Herbs Even
If You Are a Beginner*

RICHARD GREENWOOD

Introduction to Greenhouses

A greenhouse is a structure whose walls and roof are mainly composed of transparent materials, such as glass, in which plants are grown that need climatic conditions. The size of these structures ranges from small hangars to industrial buildings. A miniature greenhouse is known as a cold frame. The inside of a sun-exposed greenhouse becomes much warmer than the outside ambient temperature, thus protecting its contents in cold climates.

Many glasshouses or greenhouses are high-tech structures to produce vegetables or flowers. Glass greenhouses have equipment such as filters, heating, cooling, and lighting, and you can control it by a computer to optimize plant growth conditions. Furthermore, you can use various techniques to evaluate the degree of optimization and comfort ratio of the greenhouse microclimate (air temperature, relative humidity, and vapor pressure deficit) to reduce production risks.

- In the seventeenth century, they constructed a greenhouse with ordinary brick or wood, with a normal proportion of windows and some means of heating. When glass became available, and heating forms became more sophisticated, the greenhouse became a glass structure. A considerable increase in the availability of exotic plants in the 19th century led to strong growth of greenhouses in England and elsewhere. Major greenhouses play an important role in agriculture, horticulture, and botany, while amateurs and gardeners often use small structures.

A modern greenhouse is usually a glass or plastic structure to manage vegetables, fruit, flowers, and many plants that require special climate conditions. The basic structural forms are narrow with an A-shaped sloped roof. Sometimes individuals join two or more greenhouses, so there are fewer exterior walls, which reduces heating costs.

Greenhouses have large glass areas on both sides and roof to expose plants to natural light most of the day. Glass is the traditional material, but you can use plastic films, such as polyethylene or polyvinyl, and fiberglass also.

The greenhouse is partly warmed by the sun's rays and partly by artificial means, such as steam, hot water or circulating hot air. As a greenhouse can become too hot and too cold, a type of ventilation system is also needed; they are usually roof openings mechanically or automatically, and the final openings allow electric fans to attract and circulate air throughout the interior.

Each greenhouse model includes some temperature control features and other components to help you utilize the greenhouse's functions. Some of these components or amenities include electricity, heat, water, lighting, shelves, and benches. For example, the heating system enables you to grow your plants at any time of the year, so you don't have to worry about which season is the best for growing each crop. The lighting will enable you to walk into the garden, even in the dark, and work on the crops, including planting new ones, trimming, and cutting.

A greenhouse is a closed space used only for growing crops. Greenhouses allow temperature and humidity to be adjusted in enclosed spaces so that certain crops can grow and thrive regardless of the weather. A greenhouse is an environmental enhancement and strategic planning system that allows the cultivation of plants in climates and seasons that would not otherwise be well suited for their growth

Chapter 1: Types of Greenhouse

Structure design

Greenhouses are available in various shapes and size suitable for multiple climatic zones prevailing on the planet. Each zone requires different forms for giving favorable capable climatic conditions to the development of plants. The greatest amount of insulation possible, covering of maximum ground area for the least cost and a structurally sound facility are some of the criteria for the development of several types of greenhouse. From numerous greenhouse designs found, for example, is solarium ("lean-to'', joined to a house), even and uneven span, "hillside" and saw tooth types are as yet found all through the world. A portion of these are economically impractical and would not meet the necessities of a controlled situation; the sawtooth, be that as it may, has been used in the horticulture industry of created nations. The designs showed next are accepted by both European and American guidelines for greenhouse development. Present-day designs have followed from these first methodologies. Unsupported green-houses are usually of two types, peak rooftop (A-frame) or Arch/curvilinear. These designs are bolstered independent from anyone else; for example, no outer support is given. Arch rooftop designs are created not because of light transmission contemplations, however because of financial elements; these can be built for approximately 25% less expensive than a peak rooftop design. The Arched rooftop is effectively versatile to both unbending and adaptable covering material.

Now and again the unattached peak or Arch designs are joined to frame "frame and wrinkle" office or multi-length. This sort of arrangement is appropriate to the majority of the business greenhouses utilized for horticulture and vegetable creation. They are more affordable to assemble, monitor ground territory, and require less heating expense per ground region contrasted with remain solitary designs (Kacira).

Ridge and Furrow Configuration of Greenhouse Structures.

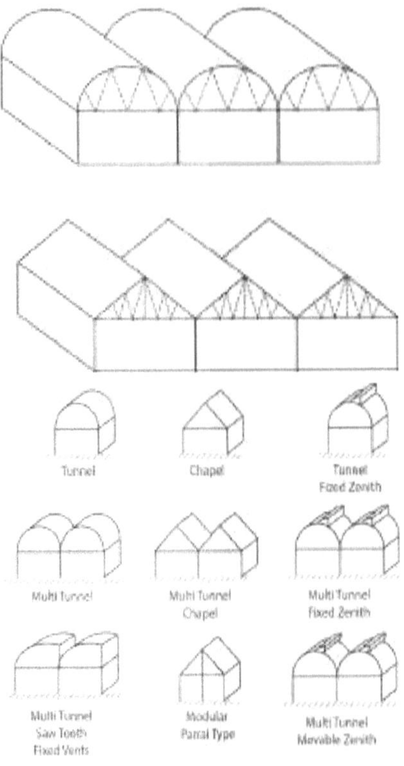

Greenhouse confirmation as per Mexican Standard (NMX-E-255-CNCP-2008)

The greenhouse structure designs, as indicated by the Mexican standard, are given above. Note that the contrast of the mark from the above mentioned yet the geometric shapes are the equivalent; a portion of these designs include a zenith or rooftop vent for accomplishing better ventilation.

Designs description

There are some greenhouse classifications as indicated by various criteria (for example, material for development, spread material sort, rooftop highlights, and so forth.). In any case, it is liked to list the most significant overlooking a few features for classification. Among the most well-known kind of greenhouses on the planet are (Bouzo and Gariglio, 2009):

Arch rooftop – or tunnel

It is portrayed by the state of its housing and its all-metal structure. The utilization of this kind of greenhouse is spreading because of its more prominent capacity to control the miniaturized scale atmosphere, its protection from high breezes and fast establishment with pre-assembled designs. The most extreme tallness of such greenhouses is between 3.5 m and 5 m. Side dividers receive statures from 2.5 m to 4 m. The width of these greenhouses is between 6 m and 9 m, and they permit a multi-range arrangement. Ventilation is through horizontal and rooftop windows.

Advantages:

High transmittance of daylight.

Great indoor air volume (high heat latency). Great protection from winds.

Thoroughly free inside space, giving simple uprooting, automated culturing, crops driving, and so forth.

Development of medium to low unpredictability (because of the accessibility of prefabricated components).

Disadvantages:

Significant expense.

They face ventilation challenges if they are worked in multi-length, and there is no rooftop vent system.

Standard peak – or house of prayer

It is perhaps the most established design, utilized in constrained harvest cultivation. The incline of the rooftop is variable as indicated by radiation and precipitation (typically changing somewhere in the range of 15∘ and 35∘). Width measurements vary somewhere in the range of 6 and 12 m (considerably higher) for variable length. The stature of the horizontal range between 2.0 m to 2.5 m and 3.0 m to 3.5 m the frame (likewise constructed lower than those shown, however, are not suggested). The ventilation of these greenhouses in a single range has no troubles, turning out to be progressively troublesome when these are canal associated.

Advantages:

Development of low to medium unpredictability.

Utilization of cheap materials relying upon the territory (eucalyptus shafts and timbers, pine, and so on.).

• Side ventilation is exceptionally simple. It is likewise simple to introduce rooftop windows.

• Suitable for both covering materials adaptable and unbending.

• It has incredible offices for depleting water.

Disadvantages:

• Ventilation issues with canal associated greenhouses.

• It has less encased volume than bent greenhouses with a similar peak stature.

• A larger number of components that decrease light transmittance (more noteworthy concealing).

• Internal bolster components thwart the development and area of crops.

Sawtooth

A variety of chapel greenhouses, which was first utilized in quite a while with exceptionally low precipitation and significant levels of radiation were greenhouses that had a solitary rooftop tilted at points going from 5° to 15°. The sidelong coupling of such started the greenhouses known as "sawtooth". The need to clear water from precipitation decided a tendency in assortment zones from the centre towards the two finishes.

Advantages:

• Construction of medium multifaceted nature.

• Excellent ventilation which varies from the multi-length house of prayer greenhouses.

• Use of suitable materials relying upon the region.

Disadvantages:

- Concealing a lot more noteworthy than a chapel because of the more prominent number of supporting basic components.

- Low volume of air encased (for a similar peak stature) than a house of prayer.

Modular Parral type

These greenhouses are originated in the region of Almería (Spain), made up of posts and wires called "parral" which are a changed form of the designs used to develop table grapevines. Right now, there is a cutting frame rendition of the first worked with aroused channels as indoor backings, the utilization of posts stay for horizontal strain holding wind loads. These greenhouses, for the most part, have a frame stature of 3.0 m to 3.5 m, the width is variable, extending inside 20 m or additionally relying upon the length. The slant is practically nonexistent, or in territories with a high water hazard, ordinarily is between 10° to 15°, which speaks to sidelong tallness of about 2.0 m to 2.3 m. It is vented uniquely through horizontal openings.

Advantages:

• Low-cost development.

• Large volume of air encased (great conduct contingent upon the heat dormancy).

• Negligible rate of rooftop components in the block attempt of light.

• High wind load obstruction.

Detriments:

Poor ventilation.

The danger of breakage by overwhelming precipitation because of the low seepage limit. Development of high unpredictability (requires specific staff).

In zones of low radiation, the low slanted rooftop speaks to the low take-up of daylight.

Venlo house

These are glass greenhouses where the boards lay on the water assortment channels; they are commonly utilized in Northern Europe. The width of every module is 3.2 m, and the dispersing between posts the longitudinal way is around 3 m. These greenhouses have no side windows (perhaps because in Holland there are very few requests for ventilation). Instead, it has rooftop windows, opening substituting (coordinated side and by the other) whose measurements are 1.5 m long and 0.8 m wide.

Advantages:

The better heat exhibition because of the kind of material utilized: glass, and unbending materials as of now.

• High level of control of natural conditions.

Detriments:

Significant expense.

The transmittance is influenced, not on account of the spread material, however by the enormous number of supporting components because of the heaviness of the spread material. Being an inflexible material, enduring quite a long while, their light transmission is influenced by dust, green growth, and so on.

Greenhouse plan by the atmosphere

Not all greenhouses are planned equivalent. A plan that functions admirably in a cool atmosphere with long virus winters, snowfall, low light and high breezes won't be the best design for a sticky, tropical atmosphere with variable light force. Various greenhouses are described by the degree of insurance from the outside condition they can offer and the ability they can give producers to control within the condition to a particular arrangement of shapes. The degree of protection required relies upon the kind of crop being developed and the neighbourhood atmosphere. The target with building any greenhouse is to discover a plan that will permit the producer to defeat the most restricting climatic issues in their specific zone and acquire the greatest development rates conceivable from their crops. The necessities of greenhouse designs because of various climatic zones that can be found the world over are (Morgan, 2012):

Dry tropical or desert atmospheres

The principle ecological dangers are high breezes vehicle drying residue or sand, which can impact the two harvests and greenhouses. Basic tents with shafts developed with high-tractable steel wires to shape an essential design over which a solitary layer of fine creepy-crawly work is extended and verified around the frames. Moist can be expanded by hazing or clouding, which likewise acts to diminish temperatures. Further developed hello there tech, PC controlled and cooled designs are additionally being used in atmospheres like this.

Subtropical desert and Mediterranean atmospheres

A design that can be heated yet at the same time keep up a cool situation in summer are fundamental. Right now atmosphere an appropriate design is the "cushion and fan" cooled plastic greenhouse with top vents and heating. Alongside concealing over the outside of the greenhouse, this creates a perfect domain during dry summer conditions.

Moist tropical atmospheres

Good tropical greenhouse designs can be as straightforward as a downpour spread or plastic rooftop with open or move upsides secured with bug work. In bigger greenhouses, the design is best planned with a "saw tooth" rooftop format which permits great venting of the sight-seeing inside the greenhouse on crisp mornings. Heating, what's more, protection isn't required, and vents can stay open. Moistening systems and air-development fans can be utilized to cool the earth inside this sort of design, and portable heat screens can be utilized to decrease approaching daylight on brilliant, cloudless days and pulled back to permit greatest light entrance under cloudy conditions. High breezes from tropical storms or sea tempests can be a significant hazard right now.

Mild atmospheres

Efficient heating of the air inside the greenhouse and protecting and keeping up this heated air is the primary thought. Cultivators need all year high development rates and most extreme crops in these situations usually select greenhouses highlighting completely clad side dividers, rooftop and side vents, permitting enormous ventilation regions and PC control of ecological equipment, for example, heaters, shade or heat screens, hazing and vents. Mild zone greenhouse designs regularly utilize plastic cladding "twin skins" where the space between the two layers of plastic is expanded, offering improved protection and better natural control.

Cold calm atmospheres

Greenhouses for this sort of condition need strong dividers and firmly built, relatively soak strong rooftops to convey snow stacks that would fall plastic film designs. These greenhouses are frequently twofold protected by introducing plastic film within dividers and situating retractable heat screens over the overhang at stud stature. To forestall heat misfortune, vents are frequently kept shut throughout the winter months.

The world agro-climatic zones show the most appropriate greenhouse design designs, considering the above data.

Most present-day hydroponic greenhouses for all atmospheres nowadays highlight a stud stature of at any rate 3.05 m and at times considerably more. Despite the sort or plan of the greenhouse or what harvest is being grown, a tall greenhouse design gives a superior situation for plants and a bigger cushion against minor changes in outside temperatures. The subsequently improved limit with regards to air development is a fundamental part of present-day greenhouse editing that has been shown to profit various crops by improving transpiration and decreasing malady. The volume of air that should be heated in cooler atmospheres can be diminished by pulling heat screens over the greenhouse rooftop around evening time and heating just under the screen, this makes an enormous protection layer over the screen and under the greenhouse rooftop, along these lines easing back the pace of Heat misfortune through the cladding (Morgan, 2012).

For improved harvest creation and quality, a cautious choice of greenhouse design, coating, and atmosphere control system is required. All greenhouses ought to be planned appropriately to withstand all conceivable burden factors for security and legitimate functionality purposes. The National Greenhouse Manufacturers Association (NGMA) distributes principles that give direction for deciding design loads for greenhouses (Kacira, 2013).

Chapter 2: Planning your Greenhouse

There are a lot of considerations to be made before you buy a greenhouse. There is a budget, but other factors may well influence your budget. If you live in a particularly cold area, then double glazing and heating are important, but in a hotter area, the primary considerations would be airflow and ventilation.

What Size to Buy

Bigger is not always best, but many people aspire to a large greenhouse. What size to buy will depend on the space you have available plus what you are planning to grow. Of course, no matter what size you buy when you start to use it you will run out of space and wish you'd bought a bigger one!

If you are buying a second-hand greenhouse or picking one up for free, then you have less choice in size and will usually make do with whatever comes up.

The most common size is 8' x 6' though you can get slightly smaller ones and very much larger ones. This is a good starter size, but you need to be aware that your space is limited and you will struggle to fit a lot in. However, it is a great size for starting seeds and growing a few tomatoes or chili plants.

Check any local planning or zoning regulations before you buy a greenhouse. If you are on an allotment, then check their rules too. The last thing you want is to put up your new greenhouse only to find you have breached a rule and then have to take it down. On allotments, you often need written permission for a greenhouse and to position it in a certain way. As to HOA's, their rules are anyone's guess so check and be certain.

I would recommend visiting a shop that sells greenhouses and walking into a few different sizes. This will help you to visualize the space better and work out which one is best for you. Just remember to avoid the sales person's charm, or you may end up with a very expensive greenhouse!

When looking for a greenhouse, you need to consider how easy it is for you to maintain and use the greenhouse. If your greenhouse takes a lot of time to maintain each year, then it means less time doing other jobs.

That's the greenhouse I inherited which, as you can see, is a marvel of British engineering. Quite how it is still standing is beyond me as I understand it is well over 20 years old, but it shows what can be made with a bit of creativity!

Positioning Your Greenhouse

Where you will put your greenhouse can influence the size, as well as other factors. You need to position it, so it gets good sun throughout the day.

Avoid north-facing slopes as the amount of light will not be sufficient. Do not build your greenhouse at the bottom of a slope as it is likely to be the location of a frost pocket, meaning cold air will gather around your greenhouse. This makes your greenhouse colder, requiring more heating and reducing the benefits you get from your greenhouse.

Though if you have no choice but to site your greenhouse facing north that is still better than not having a greenhouse at all!

Depending on your preference you may choose to align your greenhouse in one of two ways.

Firstly, you can align it so the sun tracks down one side of the greenhouse. The advantage of this is that one side gets lots of suns and the other gets less allowing you to grow plants that require less sun or need a bit of shade on the side of the greenhouse furthest from the sun.

Alternatively, you can align your greenhouse, so the sun shines on one of the small ends so the whole greenhouse gets sun throughout the day.

Which you choose is up to you, and it may be that the locations available to you in your vegetable plot influences the alignment.

As an 8' x 6' greenhouse is virtually square, the alignment to the sun is not so important. For larger greenhouses, it does become more important to ensure you maximize the sun for your plants.

Something else to consider is the direction of the prevailing wind in your area. Typically, you will position the door away from the wind. This helps secure your greenhouse and make it a little less susceptible to wind damage.

You want to position your greenhouse where it is not under trees. Should the trees lose branches, then it will damage or even destroy your greenhouse.

Ideally, you want your greenhouse located in a sheltered spot where it is not going to be subjected to high winds. This may not always be possible, but if you can do this, then it will help prevent damage in the future.

If you are planning on using an irrigation system or installing electricity, then your choice of the site needs to consider this. It needs to be somewhere that you can supply these services to without too much work or expense. If not, then you are stuck watering by hand and using paraffin or solar heaters like most gardeners!

Choosing the Best Floor

All of these decisions need making before you buy your greenhouse and this is probably one of the most controversial!

Which floor you choose will depend a lot on what you are planning on growing in your greenhouse and your environment.

Your choices are:

1. No floor, just use the soil
2. The concrete path down the middle, soil to either side
3. The concrete path down the middle, weed membrane on either side
4. Complete concrete floor

They all have their pros and cons, but it is a personal decision based on your site, budget, and available resources.

The picture is the inside of my inherited greenhouse. It contains a central paved path with weed membrane on either side on it laid on the soil.

The problem with this is that the weed membrane does not extend outside of the greenhouse, meaning the hard to reach edges become infested with weeds. This is okay on the left-hand side but the right-hand side has staged in place so is extremely hard to weed.

The lesson has been learned, and on my next greenhouse, the inside will be much more weed proof! But back to choosing the best floor for your greenhouse.

The first option is by far the easiest because you don't need to do anything. The downside of this is the weeds will love the heat in the greenhouse and will thrive. You will have a lot of weeding to do, and this can be very awkward to do when the plants are fully grown.

Some people do grow directly into the soil using bottomless pots. Just be aware that although this option is cheap, you will be battling weeds inside your greenhouse as well as outside. You also run the risk of introducing soil born pests and diseases if you do not change the topsoil in your greenhouse every year or two.

Having a paved path down the middle of your greenhouse is great as it helps with access and isn't too expensive. You can leave the soil bare on either side or cover with a weed membrane.

This method works well, as when you put staging in your greenhouse, it becomes very hard to weed underneath it.

Putting weed membrane down will be effective in keeping the weeds away providing you use a decent quality membrane. Expect to replace it every 2 to 5 years, depending on what you use as it will perish and eventually allow weeds through.

The final option is by far the best but is also the most expensive as you have to buy paving slabs for the whole greenhouse or poured concrete. With a larger greenhouse this can soon become expensive. It is also more work as you have to lay sand and hardcore as well as level the paving.

The advantage of this method is that it is a low maintenance solution. When done properly with weed membrane under the sand, you should get years of a weed-free greenhouse.

As everything will be in pots, you can also move your plants around so you can reposition them as necessary to get them more or less sun as required.

Glass vs. Polycarbonate Panes

Again this is a personal preference, and both types of the panel have their good and bad points.

Glass is the more expensive solution, and the most fragile, panes can get broken by accident or vandals and need replacing.

However, glass technology is quite advanced, and you can get some great thermally insulated glass which is ideal for colder areas or heated greenhouses.

Most greenhouses use horticultural glass which typically comes in 2' square panes so you can end up with overlapping panes. The disadvantage of this type of glass is that it breaks easily into very jagged and sharp pieces. Because of the size, the panes come in you overlap them, and over time this can become dirty and grow algae, which looks unsightly.

You can buy specially toughened glass for your greenhouse, meaning it isn't going to shatter from a simple touch. It is still breakable, but it will survive an impact from a football though a more solid ball will break it. Just be careful of the edges of toughened glass as that is its weak point. When handling this make sure you never let the edges touch a rough surface.

Plastic or polycarbonate panes are much cheaper to buy and for most applications just as good as glass. The big advantage is that they are a lot harder break which is important if you have kids as accidents do happen.

Because the polycarbonate panes are much lighter than glass, they are also more susceptible to wind damage. In high winds, they can flex and pop out of the frame!

Glass is much heavier and gives your greenhouse a more rigid structure, something that is lacking with the polycarbonate panes.

Many polycarbonate panes are slightly opaque, meaning you cannot see in or out clearly. This may not bother you, but some people don't like it, and it can reduce the amount of sunlight your plants get.

You should also be aware that most polycarbonate panes are twin-walled, meaning there are two sheets of plastic with an air gap in the middle. Over time water seeps into this gap and algae forms, which you cannot remove. This has an impact on how much light gets into your greenhouse and also looks untidy. Surprisingly, polycarbonate can cost even more than toughened glass!

Both are easy to get your hands on, being available in many glaziers. My personal preference is the plastic panes purely from the point of view that they are harder to break and less likely to smash if people throw stones at it. However, if I were to heat my greenhouse, then I would look at glass panels for better insulation and heat retention.

Half Brick Greenhouses

This type of greenhouse has several layers of bricks before the greenhouse itself starts. These are not so common these days but are still an option.

Because of the weight, you will need a more significant foundation for your greenhouse. You need to dig down about 18 inches and lay a concrete foundation which will then support the weight of the bricks and the greenhouse itself.

Also known as dwarf wall greenhouses, these harken back to Victorian times when the glass was more expensive and brick cheaper. Today, though, brick is more expensive, but the greenhouse does look great and there are some advantages!

The Victorians were masters of engineering and ingenuity, and these dwarf wall greenhouses had a very specific purpose.

The brick heats up slowly during the day than the glass which means it helps to keep the greenhouse cool. However, at night the bricks retain the heat and cool more slowly than the glass which keeps the greenhouse warm.

Another advantage is that brick doesn't break. Typically, it will be the lower panes that break as you mow or strim around the greenhouse and kick up stones.

Of course, these half brick greenhouses also look great and are a fine addition to any garden.

Wood vs. Aluminum Frames

Wooden frames look great on a greenhouse, but they are more expensive and will require regular maintenance. You will need to treat the wood every year to prevent it from rotting and keep it looking great. Eventually, though the wood will need replacing and it can be difficult and time-consuming to replace single pieces of wood.

Wooden framed greenhouses look great and when looked after will last for many years. Because of their weight and natural strength, they are less susceptible to wind damage. So if you live in an area with high winds, then it may be worth investing in a wooden frame to prevent damage to your greenhouse.

For the smaller size greenhouses, it will come as two side panels, two end panels, and two roof panels.

All you need to do is bolt it all together, though you will need help due to the weight of the wood and size of the panels.

Larger greenhouses will come with more panels. You will need to ensure you have suitable access to your greenhouse site so you can get the panels to the right place.

Aluminum frames are much cheaper to buy and will usually come flat packed, so you have to assemble it yourself. They will also usually fit in your car so you can take them home then and there rather than wait for delivery.

This does mean you can do a lot of it by yourself as it is much lighter than wood, but it is also more likely to twist. With an aluminum greenhouse, you need to ensure that the greenhouse is square and level, which can take time.

Although much more affordable than wood, aluminum is a lot lighter. This means you need to take extra care to secure it to the ground to prevent wind damage. High winds will tear an aluminum greenhouse to pieces, twisting the frame and shattering the glass. When properly secured though it can survive all but the most severe storms.

Some greenhouses come with powder-coated frames which gives them a nice color. A powder-coated frame will last a good ten years without any treatment and can last 15 to 25 years without any need to paint, which surely is good news for us all!

Powder coating is a chemical process which coats the aluminum frame with colored powder. This is baked on. The range of colors available is good though you will need to get your greenhouse from a supplier that offers this service. You can expect to pay a premium price for this coating though.

Which you choose is up to you, but most of us will go for aluminum frames purely from an affordability point of view.

Greenhouses vs. Polytunnels

In many ways, a polytunnel is very similar to a greenhouse in that it insulates your plants from the weather and helps them thrive.

Polytunnels are typically made from plastic or aluminum pipes and covered with a strong plastic sheeting.

These are much cheaper than greenhouses, but they aren't quite the same.

A polytunnel is much weaker than a greenhouse and more likely to be damaged in high winds. It also does not provide the same level of insulation as a greenhouse. It is still excellent for growing plants and keeping them warm, but in the colder months, it will be harder to heat and keep warm.

A lot of serious growers will start their plants off in a greenhouse before moving them into a polytunnel to complete their growing season. Frost tender plants are then often moved back into the greenhouse in winter for that extra protection from the weather.

A polytunnel is a good starter for growing with many similar considerations to a greenhouse. Remember to buy the strongest you can afford and secure it against the wind fully.

Chapter 3: Greenhouse Equipment (Climate Control, Lighting, Irrigation Systems, etc.)

Technology advancement has made owning and running greenhouses simpler than ever before. Options of environmental control help the professional horticulturist or home gardener by automatically adjusting light intensity, humidity, and temperature from a remote location or within the greenhouse. A system of environmental control would enhance plant life within the structure by offering a continually monitored atmosphere, producing a more consistent yield.

You can automate your greenhouse environmental control systems according to your requirements. Greenhouse accessories are pre-set in phases in line with the plant's needs and gardener's choice. These systems present the most significant advantage by providing the facility to control light intensity, adjust humility, adjust the temperature, and monitor the atmosphere, to mention some of the operations.

Accessories Controlled

Cooling systems, heating systems, fogging, systems, misting systems, vents, and fans are all controlled by control systems. The operations could be very straightforward and offer an immense benefit to keeping your greenhouses in ideal shape.

The first phase of execution could be as simple as on/off switch to control fans circulation. By semi-automating a control system using a timing device, a thermostat, or a humidistat, the accessories will run only when necessary; this saves energy and reduces the operating costs. A fully automated system can be controlled through a cell phone, by remote programming system on a PC, or semaphore, saving a considerable amount of time. The fully automated system could be programmed to keep a particular set of conditions for stable plant comfort, putting into consideration the circumstances outside the structure, which might affect the growth of plants.

Advantages of Automated System

Improve Vegetation Quality: Mimicking a colder night temperature, boosts the quality of vegetation as it more directly simulates the natural environment. Precise humidity and temperature control offer consistent growing conditions to improve production and quality.

Reduce costs of fuel: Lowering the temperature of a greenhouse at night when eighty percent of the heating takes place, lessens the consumption of energy. Centralizing temperature sensors, controlling them with a single unit, prevents cooling and heating systems from running concurrently.

Increase Production: An automated system permits you to focus on growing the plants, not adjusting settings.

Advanced Accessories

Additionally, to regular greenhouses accessories, environmental control systems could be programmed to contain advanced elements like remote programming, semaphore, soil sensors, photo and light sensors, drip systems, foggers, and coolers. Your time can now be spent tending to plants instead of messing with their growing environment. Asides the time and cost-effectiveness of the greenhouse control system, Mother Nature will also benefit. Control systems lessen the use of chemicals to aid the growth of plants as the environment is more closely adjusted to produce the perfect condition and reduce energy costs and waste. Here are some of the greenhouses advance accessories:

Greenhouse Benches

These benches will make performing gardening functions stress-free. Whether you're transplanting, pruning, potting, or washing farm produce, benches provide alternatives in space and height utilization. The greenhouse benches are built to complement any existing or new structure. The polyethylene grid-top and galvanized mesh offer both good drainage and air circulation while giving room for light to pass through to the plants underneath.

Raised Seedling Beds

Seeding beds are another fantastic accessory for greenhouses. Unlike conventional greenhouse benches, they extend growing beyond only pots. A seedling bed is about six inches deep and is supported on four legs. It is often filled with soil for growing plants. Seedling beds are the ideal way to bring a vegetable garden or flower bed straight into the greenhouse. With this, you don't have to get on your knees to plant and tend the garden as the bed is raised.

Gravel Bench

This is specially used to produce moisture. This type of bench is tailored for use in greenhouses or with plants such as orchids. You can use a fixed bench built with a metal top rather than a conventional mesh top. To apply, fill the top of the bench with gravel and water to create a source of moisture for the flowers.

Grow Lights

A greenhouse such as a lean-to with low light and conventional side walls or ceiling wouldn't generate the amount of natural heat needed by specific plants. The addition of grow light is a simple solution. There are also conversion lighting kits. The grow light permits high-pressure sodium light bulb and metal halide to be interchanged. You can rotate the bulbs as the greenhouse advances and plant selections change. These lightings promote new growth and keep plants healthy. There are several forms of grow light in the market nowadays; for example, compact fluorescent produces light and incandescent light. Most of these models may not last long and are dangerous if water comes in contact with their bulbs. I recommend lights featuring high-pressure sodium or metal halide bulbs:

I. High-Pressure Sodium

A high-pressure sodium (HPS) bulb has a yellow glow that isn't as visually pleasing as the blue light metal halide produce. The bulbs can last for twenty-four thousand hours (about five years). HPS bulbs are suggested for greenhouses with enough lighting but want to produce more flowering plants, fruits, or vegetables.

II. Metal Halide

Metal halide bulbs emit a blue tint that mimics real sunlight and can last for twenty thousand hours. Plants become fuller when placed under a metal halide bulb. If you want to elongate daytime growing hours, the ideal option is the metal halide system as you can turn the light on before sunset and again a few hours after sunset.

Heat Mats

When propagating plants or starting seeds, a heat mat will be a useful propagation tool. Plug the waterproof rubber mat into an outlet to generate heat. The heat will produce warm seedling trays that will help to grow plants faster.

Plant Hangers

For you to take advantage of all the available space within your greenhouse, plant hangers will help just in achieving that. You can hang orchid boxes along with hanging flower baskets. You can also hang tomatoes pot if you wish. You can as well install multiple rods in your greenhouse to offer ample space, and hang many baskets from it for an ever-growing plant assortment.

Advanced Ventilation

Eave vents and ridge vents are a crucial part of any functioning greenhouse with a serviceable passive system of ventilation. When the air is not vented, it turns out to be stale, stagnant and gives room for diseases to breed. To avoid this scenario, you need to install eave vents and ridge vents in your greenhouse. Both systems work similarly but on different parts of the greenhouse. The two units are operable panels of glass-enclosed within a frame separate from the structural framework of the greenhouse. The vent will open by a motor that is dampness-resistance, or manually with the help of a rod operator. It will open to a specific direction and give room for air into the building. Both systems have screens that prevent debris and insects from gaining entrance to the greenhouse.

Ridge Vent

The ridge vent is essential for a greenhouse. Warm air upsurges and builds up at the top of the greenhouse. When you open the ridge vents, the warm air breaks out, and fresh, cold air breaks in. The ridge vents will also enable air circulation. If there is light wind outside, it will get into the structure and help in circulating the air; this will lessen the spread of diseases. If your greenhouse is in use of exhaust fan/intake louvers, the ridge vents will help in getting rid of hot air, so fresh air can go into the building.

Eave Vents

The eave vents are situated on the walls of the structure and would also open. And this allows fresh, cold air into the building. The air would spread through the room and reduce the temperature. It makes the house calmer and helps lessen the emergence of disease in greenhouse plants. You can also add rain sensors to the units so the when rain or snow hits the vents, they close automatically. If you operate an environmental control system in your greenhouse, you can program the ridge vents into your specified system. Without aeration, your greenhouse would become a glass box filled with stagnant air.

Advance Watering Systems

The perfect methods of providing your plants with essential sustenance are watering systems. Watering with the hand can become time-consuming and tedious as your plant collection grows. An automated system of watering is well-suited for plants that require high humid environments. There are several available watering systems. For example, a misting system that sprays a mist and makes the air to be saturated. The water drips are larger than the ones provided by a fogging system.

You can fit all the systems with different nozzle heads and utilize them within the same greenhouse. There are various flow rates for different nozzles so that you can create poles-apart zones. You can use a larger fluid nozzle to make sure seedlings don't dry out, while a small amount of water might be perfect for mature plants. You can program all the systems to work on a timer to control the amount of water that reaches the plants

Drip Misting System

You can use a drip misting system for a slow release of water. This system is perfect if you travel frequently or you have busy schedules. This system is run in such a way that it provides constant water supply to individual plants. You can fill the tubes and rearrange the holes.

Riser Misting System

This system is programmed for the utmost flexibility, and it's mobile. Therefore if you regularly change the layout of your greenhouse, riser misting system will be your best option. You can place this system anywhere on the bench and move to a different area whenever you like.

Suspended Misting System

These misting systems are lifted above the benches of the greenhouse to give room for unhindered bench space. In the suspended misting system, you will directly insert the nozzles into the water source. The building runs the benches length, and it's suspended from a jack chain that you can position at any height you prefer.

Retractable Hose Reels

Water is unavoidable in any greenhouse. If you don't use a system or watering can, then the probable option is the hose. Most gardeners are aware that hose can be bulky and occupy valuable space. When it uses a hose holder, and the unit usually twists and folds under the hose weight. To prevent these, a retractable hose reel that is mounted to a wall or rafter will help. A simple tow of the entire length of the hose retracts unit will provide a neat appearance and prevent tripping hazards. The reel turns left and right, giving maneuverability all through the greenhouse. You can also mount these units outside a greenhouse by attaching them to a garage or home.

Greenhouse Shelving

Shelving options offer additional growing and storage space for any greenhouse type. You can attach a shelf to the rafters in front of glass windows or add it to a solid wall. If there is enough space, you stack shelving on a wall. You can use this shelving for any conventional or glazed building, as they are designed to go with the aesthetics of the environment. You can turn a bay window into a miniature greenhouse by adding shelving. Garden windows usually contain several shelves for growing plants.

Best materials for shelving:

Glass

Glass is conventionally used in garden windows since it gives room for the sun to get to the shelves, and provided that you use saucers under the plants; it requires a minimal level of glass cleaning. The glass shelves would be the perfect artistic match to the façade of the window.

Wood

Wood is another aesthetically attractive option for shelving. I recommend cedar or mahogany since they can endure humidity and moisture. Once you have stained the wood, it will look like a conventional English greenhouse. Using wooden shelves will reduce sun to lower shelves, which is best for shade-loving plants like orchids.

Metal

Metal is solid and allows for the flow of air into the plant's bottom. The aluminum mesh is an excellent option for bonsai that usually demands the movement of air to thrive. Metal won't warp or rust and is a handy option for any greenhouse.

Polyethylene

Polyethylene is almost the same with metal shelving in form and benefits. The main variation is that the former is plastic with reprocessed substance. The polyethylene is black and covers dirt quickly, while metal shelving is silver.

Bench Shelving

The lower bench shelves for greenhouses are handy for plants that flourish in the shade or minimal sun conditions. These benches can be about eighteen inches deep and position beneath the existing greenhouse benches. Addition of the lower shelf increases the available growing space and provides added storage space for equipment and supplies.

Shelf Supports

The shelving supports could be either a decorative corner or a simple metal bar. Decorative corners are an ideal option when aesthetics matters. You can attach a metal bar from the above or beneath the shelf to create a hanging shelf. They are available in different forms that mimic the traditional structural design and English greenhouse.

Chapter 4: How to Build Your Greenhouse

Now that you understand what a greenhouse is and what you need to get started with planting, you need to know what materials you need to build your greenhouse. This sounds like a massive feat, and in some respects, it is. Depending on the size and style of the greenhouse you want this can either be a really hard part of the job or a really easy part of the job.

Keep in mind that you don't have to do all this building yourself. There are plenty of companies out there that can assist you from start to finish. This doesn't mean you don't have a say in how your greenhouse is built, it simply means you're requesting the help you need. There's zero shame in admitting when you need help and letting the experts come in to help you. There are some steps that you can follow when it comes to building your greenhouse. Even if you are having other people build it for you (like a reputable greenhouse company) read these steps so that you can have a big hand in the personal design and construction of your greenhouse.

1.   You need to first choose what kind of greenhouse you want to build. This includes the style and the frame of your greenhouse. There are dozens upon dozens of types of greenhouses, and you must decide which one will suit your needs best. There is no point in creating a budget for yourself until you've chosen what type of greenhouse because this can impact the cost of the building.

2.   Once you have a clear image of what you want your greenhouse to look like, you want to make sure that it is functional and long-lasting. Sometimes you might even want it to look a specific way. That's okay. This is where you get to have fun and customize your greenhouse to you. You get to choose the type of doors you want in your greenhouse and the hardware that is used to build it. A word of caution: make sure that the doors are quality and well-insulated because you don't want them messing with your greenhouse climate. The hardware side of things means the type of material you are going to have held your greenhouse in one piece. Any greenhouse you build needs to have all the correct brackets, bolts, and other hardware items to ensure that it remains together no matter the weather outside.

3.   You need to decide what coverage you are going to go with next. Your

budget and greenhouse needs will play a role in what type of covering you choose. They can vary in thickness and material type. However, keep in mind your covering needs to be durable for all weather conditions. You don't want extreme winds to tear into your covering. You can install this on your own if you choose, or you can have someone do it for you.

4.   When it comes to building a greenhouse, you cannot skip out on things such as ventilation or cooling systems. Your ventilation system should probably cool your greenhouse so that your plants don't overheat from excessive levels of heat. You could even try and use shading to your best advantage to cool your greenhouse down. Your ventilation needs will vary depending on the size of your greenhouse.

5.   Once you have ventilation picked out you need to decide on what type of heating system you are going to use. Climate control is about more than merely cooling things down. Your heating option might be using natural gas, oil heaters, water heaters, propane heaters, convection tubing, or any of the other various heating methods employed in greenhouses. It's up to you to decide which one matches your budget and your routine.

6.   You already know that maintaining control over the heating and cooling in your greenhouse is essential to providing your plants with the proper climate that they require. You want your greenhouse to be energy-efficient in a perfect world but also for it to be functional. You can use a thermostat or even computer programs to help you maintain control of your greenhouse climate. Greenhouse climate controls are normally very user-friendly so you shouldn't have to worry about it being over complicated. Make sure you choose the right environmental control regulator to suit your needs and expertise level.

7.   As a newbie when it comes to greenhouses, there's a lot to keep in mind. You ultimately have to decide what is worthwhile to have with you when you start in your greenhouse — don't worry, mistakes can be corrected at later dates. Some of the things that can help a novice in the field of greenhouse gardening are items like a CO2 generator and irrigation systems. The CO2 generator will make sure your plants are getting what they need to maintain their growth. Having a system to irrigate your plants can ensure they get their needed water (however, you can also do this by hand if you prefer). There are lots of different systems out there to help you maintain perfect

conditions in a greenhouse, but they are not all necessary for your specific needs. Weed out the ones you need from the ones you don't to minimize your costs.

8.   You might not immediately think about benches in your greenhouse; however, they are a nice added feature that provides you comfort in your greenhouse. Benching can be used to store your plants, or even for you to have a place to sit in your greenhouse.

9.   Once you know everything that you need and want for your greenhouse it's time to place an order for the materials. You can either do this yourself and have it delivered for you to build or you can order them through a company that will come and set the greenhouse up for you.

10.   When you're all done you go ahead and build your greenhouse. It is useful to buy all your materials from one place because they can often provide you with instruction manuals on your build to better assist you in putting the greenhouse together.

Side note: Before adding a greenhouse to your property make sure that you have consent to build from any local authorities that you need it from and that you understand the possible tax implications it may or may not have for you.

Tips to Building Your Greenhouse

No matter how prepared you think you might be, there is always something that blindsides you, that you were unprepared for, and that you might have had no clue about.

Building a greenhouse might appear to be a daunting task, and it comes with its own sets of challenges. However, it doesn't have to be as difficult as it first appears. Keep these tips in mind when you get ready to build your greenhouse to avoid any major mistakes when you first start.

Before you do anything, triple check the size of the area that you want to build in and then think about spacing in your greenhouse. Make the best use of your space and don't overbuild to where your yard is crowded. A smaller greenhouse will still provide you with a yield of fruits and vegetables that you can use to feed your family. There are many options and bigger isn't always better when it comes to greenhouses. For example, if this is your very first time building and working with a greenhouse then you might decide to start small — even if your space allows for a larger greenhouse. There are two things to keep in mind with this. The first is that smaller greenhouses can present more of a challenge when attempting to regulate the climate. The second thing I want you to remember is that you can always expand your greenhouse when the time is right for you. So, don't get too hooked on if you chose the wrong size greenhouse in the end. Adjustments later on in the game are still possible.

The ideal greenhouse for the family grower will roughly be 6 feet by 12 feet.

When you have considered your space and the size of the greenhouse that you want to build it is also important to keep in mind the area you want to build it. Remember that the south side of your home will get the best sun exposure which will be beneficial to your greenhouse. In cases where the southern side of your home won't do, you can use the western side as your next best plan.

However, there is more than the sun to consider when you are placing your greenhouse in your yard. For example, during the middle of the snow, you might be more inclined to pop into the greenhouse to get some vegetables for dinner if it was closer to a door in your home. See, there's a lot to consider?

Ideally, the area you place your greenhouse in will also be an area with proper drainage. It can also be useful to add additional protection to your greenhouse by placing it close to a fence or shrubbery that will act as a shield against winds.

Do you use a kit from a company or do you build it all yourself from start to finish? While the greenhouse kit might seem higher in price than doing it all yourself, you might be saving yourself time and money in the long run by having everything you need in front of you with a map to put it together.

This ultimately comes down to your expertise in building and your comfort level ensuring that everything is put together correctly for your greenhouse.

I cannot stress enough how important it is to make sure that both your ventilation and heating systems are up to par and working as they should be. You want to regulate the temperature in your greenhouse which means that you need to make sure that your ventilation system can release the excess heat and moisture before it destroys your crop.

The roof provides its series of issues to be concerned about. Most greenhouses have peaked roofs and this is for a variety of reasons. However, for those that live in snowy climates, the main reason is so that the snow doesn't gather and collapse your roof. You can combat this if you choose to go for other roof styles such as the dome. You merely need to make sure that there is plenty of pitch on the roof to prevent snow and ice from collecting all in one area.

Flooring is another aspect of your greenhouse. Do you see where every aspect of your greenhouse can be personally tailored to your preferences? While gravel flooring is best for beginners since it is low maintenance and provides great and simple drainage, some people prefer to use concrete tiling in their greenhouses.

Finally, you need to think about how you are going to get the sun's rays into your greenhouse and to your plants. There is a wide range of materials that you can use for greenhouse windows, doors, and roofs. For example, there is glass, polycarbonate, and plastic sheeting specifically designed for greenhouses.

The material you use will be decided by your budget and what you prefer to work with. Glass will easily be both the heaviest and most expensive of all your material options. Polycarbonate that is used in greenhouses can be likened to plexiglass. The polycarbonate is specially treated to make sure that it doesn't wear down due to the sun's ultraviolet rays. This will be your middle-range product because it remains more costly than the greenhouse plastic sheeting and it can be more difficult to install as well. However, you need to consider where you live and the weather you experience because the polycarbonate will hold up better to extreme weather than the plastic sheeting will.

Plastic sheeting is a cheaper and viable option for your greenhouse. The biggest thing to keep in mind with this is that you have bought the sheeting from a company that specifically manufactured it for greenhouse use. That means it should have ultraviolet protection because it will ensure that your sheeting has a longer life while you use it. Like other materials, you will find that you can also get plastic sheeting in different thicknesses. It's good to understand your greenhouse needs because the thicker sheeting will hold up better in detrimental weather, but it will let less light into your greenhouse as a result.

How to Expand a Smaller Greenhouse

Greenhouse expansion is not as uncommon as you might initially think it is. Often new growers get the hang of what they are doing, and their greenhouse space quickly becomes too small for their needs. If you're feeding your family or a community with your greenhouse, then over time you might want to have more space to include a wider variety of fruits and vegetables. Sometimes the expansion of your greenhouse goes beyond simply making a few spacing adjustments and you end up needing to physically expand it.

This can be a difficult process. Especially when your greenhouse is already set up and functioning perfectly. You know now that there are so many systems to consider when you start talking expansion and the first will be your heating and ventilation system. If you feel like expansion is over your head or skill abilities — because let's face it many of us are better gardeners than we are builders — then reach out to your local greenhouse company and see if they can help you with the designs and building. This doesn't mean that your input goes away, simply that you are handing over the building to a more experienced team. If you feel like you know your greenhouse inside and out and the best person for the job is, of course, yourself then go for it. Regardless of whether you do it yourself or get a company to help you, your expansion process will look something like this:

• First, establish what size you want your expanded greenhouse to be. Keep in mind that this might not be the last time you have your greenhouse expanded so please be aware of that and keep space allotted for potential growth in the future. It helps to build your greenhouse expansion slightly bigger than what you think you will need at this moment. This allows you space for future growth within your greenhouse as well and prolongs the time between possible greenhouse expansions.

• When you look at space and size, you also need to plan for the best outcome for your plant's growth. This means that you want to ensure your greenhouse is running at its best climate levels to continue with the proper production of your crops. This is where you consider all the extra systems like vents, ventilation systems, material types, style and build of the greenhouse to promote the environment you want inside for your plants.

• It's great to think about expansion in terms of what we are bringing in that is new to the scene, however, you must also bear in mind what you already have and what to do with those items. Some of the systems you have in place for your greenhouse will still be sufficient to run and protect your plants even with the expansion. Other systems might need to be updated, replaced, or duplicated to maintain the proper climate for your old plants and the new ones coming in. Get a second opinion because this is where your expansion can become costly and you want to make sure that you are doing it the right way.

• There's a lot to consider and do before physically expanding your greenhouse. Part of that is double-checking the regulations of where you live. Sometimes you might need to speak to a building inspector or get another permit to build for the expansion. You don't want to expand and unknowingly break any laws that force you to tear down all of your hard work. So, acquaint yourself with all regulations about your greenhouse building and plan accordingly.

• The other caveat is that with an expansion you need to keep in mind you will produce a bigger yield.

While you expand your greenhouse, there might be a temporary change to your climate and this could impact your plants. During this time you need to keep a closer eye on your fruits, vegetables, flowers, and herbs to make sure that they are receiving everything they need during this time of transition.

Once you start on the expansion and you have the minor details sorted out you will discover that it is much the same process as it was when you were building your greenhouse. Some materials such as glass will be more difficult and expensive to expand than plastic sheeting.

Chapter 5: Good Plants for Greenhouse (Vegetables, Fruits, Flowers and Herbs)

Before we get down to talking about the fruits, herbs, and vegetables that you can grow in your garden, you might need to know about two vital terms.

Annuals

These are plants that transform from seed to flower and back to seed all within a single growing season. If you visit the market for seeds, then you might not always find true annuals. If you got yourself a true annual, then it should complete its entire life cycle within a single year. The leaves, stem, and root of the plant die every year. You might have to replace the seeds every year during springtime.

Benefits of Growing Annuals

- Annuals are efficient plants. They grow quickly and hence, you can collect the fruits (or vegetables) of your harvest quickly. Start growing them and within a year, you will be using them in your food.

- Annuals typically cost less than perennials. If you have enough annuals, then not only will you spend less on them, but you will have a large number of ingredients to work with by the end of the year.

- It is also easier to grow annuals. For most annuals, you plant them (ensuring that the soil and garden conditions are ideal), ensure they have adequate sunlight and water them. You might have to make changes to your greenhouse environment based on upcoming seasons. But you will only be making the changes once since you are going to harvest your plants by the end of the year. In the case of perennials, you need to make changes to your greenhouse year after year to ensure that they grow properly.

Image: You can harvest annuals year after year.

Cons of Growing Annuals

- Remember how I mentioned that you might have to make changes to your greenhouse for upcoming seasons? It is important, nay, almost imperative that you are prepared for upcoming seasons, especially winter. Annuals are sensitive to the cold and if you are not careful, you might lose them during the cold parts of the year.

- Annuals attract more pests than perennials, including slugs, aphids, and other insects.

- If you are the kind of person who does not have a lot of time to spend in the garden, then you might have difficulty focusing on annuals. They require constant attention.

Perennials

These are persistent plants that require multiple growing seasons to fully mature. Every winter, the top part of the plant might die off (though this is not always the case) and then regrow once again from the root system during spring. You can harvest multiple times by using a perennial plant.

Benefits of Growing Perennials

- Perennial plants are low maintenance in the long run. Once you have set the right conditions and ensure that they adjust to the climate, you don't need to check on them as frequently as you would annuals.

- Because it takes longer to harvest perennials, they can enhance the beauty of your garden. At the end of the day, you might not be looking to just grow plants; you might also be thinking of creating a beautiful space in your garden.

- Perennials are also good for the soil. They leave behind nutritious soil once they are removed. In some cases, you can plant new crops on the soil that you used to grow perennials.

Cons of Growing Perennials

- You need to wait for the harvest. Annuals will be ready with their products within a year. With perennials, it's not always the case. Some perennials even take several years before they begin to yield anything. A good example of such a perennial is asparagus.

- You cannot place perennials anywhere in your garden. They occupy space for a long time, which means that you need to make sure that you have space for annuls. If you are only growing perennials, then you will have to wait a long time before your first harvest.

- Some perennials can turn to weeds easily. One has to be careful when picking perennials to make sure that they have chosen the right plant for their garden.

Fruits

Imagine plucking a fruit grown in your garden using ideal conditions. The fruit is fully ripe and warmed by the sun. And it is in your hands right now. The flavor is going to be more delicious compared to the ones you find in the supermarket. That is the kind of fruit you are going to grow in your garden. Of course, planning to grow the fruit is one thing, but growing it is another.

Fruits require less work compared to vegetables. Once they are planted, the trees or bushes will keep producing year after year. The pruning process can sometimes be frustrating at first, but it gets less complicated and difficult the more you do it. Eventually, you will be making fewer mistakes in future pruning processes.

Pruning is the process of removing certain parts of the plants, such as a bud or an extra branch, to maintain the health of the plant. Pruning is also done for aesthetic reasons, such as removing an unwanted leaf or two to make the overall presentation of your plants better.

You can choose a wide variety of fruits to work with or based on a specific color (if you are planning to arrange your garden using a specific aesthetic plan).

You can also choose between cool-season crops or warm-season plants.

Here are some cool-season crops that you can work with:

- Honeycrisp apples

- Pears

- Apricots

- Cherries

- Cherry plums

Warm-season plants:

- Kumquats

- Pomelos

- Avocados

- Passion fruits

- Guavas

- Kiwis

- Mandarin oranges

- Lemons

- Winter squash

Easy Fruits to Grow in a Garden

If you are unsure about what fruits are the easiest to grow in your garden, then perhaps this list might help you.

Strawberries

When freshly picked from the garden, these citrus fruits are juicy and perfect when eaten by themselves or in a smoothie. These fruits are so versatile that they can be grown in hanging baskets, raised beds, gardens or even indoor pots. Strawberries grow well in sunshine and soil that has a proper drainage system.

Raspberries

These fruits can be grown in small clumps throughout your garden or containers. Raspberries are not too demanding and can be harvested starting from late summer to early fall.

Blueberries

These plants provide beautifully scented and nutritious berries before late summer. They are perfect in containers, but you can grow them in your garden to add color to it. You should ideally grow them in moist and acidic soil, so prepare to have sulfur with you. Try to look for self-pollinating blueberries since they allow you to only need one plant to produce many fruits. It takes a while to fruit blueberries since you will be able to harvest them after 3 years. However, you can always add them to your garden to throw in a splash of warm colors. There is something beautiful about entering a garden with blueberry plants. Blueberries are one of the few plants that you can water with rainwater.

Figs

Want to bring the flavors of the Mediterranean to your garden? Then you cannot go wrong with figs. These sweet, chewy, and creamy fruits are easy to maintain in your garden. They love sunshine and warmth. It is best to grow them when their roots are restricted if you are planning to grow them in containers like a raised bed. Otherwise, you can use the plant of your choice for your garden. You might need to wait a little while to fruit the figs since they start to truly grow during fall and won't be ready for fruiting until the following summer.

Image: Strawberries are one of the easiest fruits to grow. Besides, who does not like strawberries?

Gooseberries

These fruits are succulent and hardy. They are low-maintenance and they make a unique ingredient to savory sauces. They prefer fertile soil and you have to keep them in semi-shade. Make sure that you keep them watered when you spot them ripening. They can be combined in many foods or eaten raw.

Apples

What can you say about this popular fruit that hasn't been saying a thousand times already? It has its adage. You can grow a wide variety of apples, depending on your preference. You need to maintain well-drained soil, but do not choose sandy soil for the purpose or you might not grow the apples well. Make sure that you prune the fruits every winter so that you avoid stunted growth. You can also plant two different kinds of apples and they might pollinate each other, making it easier to work with them.

Blackberries

The best part about these fruits is that they are adaptable. They can grow in almost any soil with little attention required from your side. Beware of the fact that these fruits come with thorns. But, you can always make use of a thornless variety like the apache group of blackberries.

Honeyberries

These fruits are hardy and tough, but they are packed with nutrients. To grow them properly, make sure that you have well-drained soil and provide adequate sunlight. Because of their toughness, you don't have to constantly pamper them. They are quite capable of growing without too much supervision. I recommend growing them in pairs since it increases pollination between them.

Goji Berries

These fruits have a liquorice flavor. They can withstand coastal conditions where there is constant wind. It is important to provide them with proper sunshine and you should only harvest them when they are fully ripened.

Currants

You can choose from red, white or black currants. They not only make delicious snacks, but you can turn them into jellies and jams. They require full sun, but they also need proper shade. Provide them with around 6 hours of sunlight and then place them in the shade.

Vegetables

The advantages of growing vegetables in your greenhouse or garden are threefold:

Advantage #1: Flavor

They taste better. When you grow your vegetables and start enjoying them in your meals, chances are that you are going to find it difficult to go back to supermarket bought foods. Additionally, to increase commercial yield, many producers use the process of hydroponics, where the roots are left dangling in the water. While hydroponics technology is not harmful, it does not produce vegetables with full flavors. The vegetables appear softer than they should and are almost tasteless. You can also pick vegetables that you grow at the peak of their ripeness, which is not true for vegetables that you find in the supermarket. When picked at the right time, you can enjoy home-grown ingredients before their sugars convert to starch and they lose some of their flavors.

Advantage #2: Nutrition

When you grow vegetables in your garden, they tend to be more nutritious. You grow these vegetables carefully, monitoring them at each stage of their growth. They are provided with the right amount of sunlight and water. Once they have ripened, you immediately pick fresh produce and use them for food. In supermarkets, you are not always getting fresh produce. Some of the produce is stored for weeks before it makes it to the market shelves.

Advantage #3: Variety

There is a greater opportunity to have more variety of vegetables, even when you have seasonal restrictions. Supermarkets bring better quality foods if they fit a particular season. For example, you find good quality sprouts in July and high-quality tomatoes during December. With your garden, you do not have to face such restrictions. No matter when your vegetables ripen, you are ready to harvest them and enjoy their flavors.

Choosing Vegetables

Despite the variety of vegetables presented to you, there is still the matter of picking which variety to grow. I would suggest picking those types that are not easily available in the shops, such as purple-podded French beans rather than the usual green variety, or elephant garlic rather than the regular type of garlic you find everywhere. By choosing a unique plant, you can experiment with not just plant type, but with flavors as well. If you feel that you would rather not take the risk of growing unknown varieties of foods, then you could try growing them alongside the readily available types. For example, grow elephant garlic along with regular garlic. Since you are growing two vegetables of the same type, your gardening methods will be the same for both types.

Most of the vegetables that you might grow to belong to two main categories; warm-season vegetables and cold-season one. The time of planting for each vegetable depends on weather conditions. You need to know what conditions the vegetables can tolerate. Cold-season vegetables usually grow best in early spring or during late summer. Some even grow during late autumn, when the weather has cooled down a bit. On the other hand, warm-season vegetables are ideally grown during late spring or summer. They can also be grown during early autumn when the weather has heated up a bit.

Image: Choose vegetables carefully. Take into consideration factors such as climate into consideration, among others.

If you are growing cool-season crops, then you have to make sure that they mature when the weather is cool, otherwise, they might go to seed. Warm-season crops must begin to grow after the end of winter. In some cases, gardeners look for the last frost of winter and check if warm-season crops are growing. If they are, then the gardeners will have a good harvest. If they don't, then they have to find another solution.

If you are planning to grow cool-season crops, then you should plant them in a temperature range of 40-50°F. When they start growing, then the ideal temperature range for their growth should be 70-75°F. Cool-weather crops do not produce well if the temperature during the day reaches 80°F or higher.

Some of the cool-season vegetables that you can grow are:

- Parsley

- Peas

- Broccoli

- Brussels sprouts
- Cabbage
- Kohlrabi
- Leeks
- Onions
- Spinach
- Turnips
- Radishes
- Rhubarb
- Rutabagas
- Asparagus
- Collards
- Garlic
- Horseradish
- Kale

When it comes to warm-season crops, they grow best at a temperature range of 65-86°F. However, try to maintain a temperature of at least 74°F.

Some warm-season vegetables that you can grow are:

- Sweet corn
- Tomatoes
- Cucumbers
- New Zealand spinach
- Muskmelons
- Okra
- Peppers

- Pumpkins

- Squash

- Snap beans

- Eggplant

- Lima beans

- Sweet potatoes

Whether you choose cool-season or warm-season vegetables, make sure that your greenhouse is ready for the vegetable. Prepare the soil, remove any weeds, and check for pests as well.

Herbs

Want a little oregano to add a beautiful scent to your food? Want to make use of fresh chives that simply enhance the flavor of your food? Or are you looking for some parsley to add to your pasta?

Image: Herbs are easy to grow in the garden.

Herbs are a wonderful addition to any food. Whether you want to use them to enhance the fragrance of the food or you are looking to create a variety in flavors, herbs are your best to creating wholesome and delicious food.

Herbs are famous for their perfumes. Many herbs are used for medicinal purposes, but a fair share of those that have a wonderful scent is used in the culinary world. Aromatic oregano, mint and lemon balm are just a few of the herbs that you might find in many kitchens.

Herbs are also well-known for attracting beneficial wildlife to your garden. If you have herbs planted next to your fruits or vegetables, then you are only going to attract those pests that are useful for you, such as certain species of spiders. Herbs also help mask the smell of fruits and vegetables, keeping away those pests that could cause harm in your garden. Most notably, gardeners who face problems with aphids grow herbs in their garden. The scent of the herbs easily keeps away the creatures.

But there is another reason for growing herbs in your garden. Despite their benefits, they can be quite expensive to purchase, especially when you are trying to get large quantities.

Which is why, if you choose to plant your herbs, then you are going to have a plentiful supply of herbs all summer.

Planting Herbs

When it comes to herbs, there are no set seasons perfect for planting them. You can plant your herbs during any season. You just have to make sure that the soil does not get too wet and cold. Your only focus should be on the type of herb. Are you planning to grow annuals or perennials? If you are planning to grow both, then what ratio of annuals would you like against perennials?

You might also think of which herb to grow. Here is a list of herbs you can work with.

Annual Herbs

- Basil

- German Chamomile

- Summer Savory

- Parsley

- Dill

- Chervil

- Cilantro/Coriander

Perennial Herbs

- Catnip (if you have feline overlords in the house, I'm sure they will appreciate a little catnip from their "hooman" servants)

- Chicory

- Lemon Grass

- Mint

- Oregano

- Roman Chamomile

- Lovage

- Marjoram

- Caraway

- Feverfew

- Sorrel

- Tarragon

- Winter Savory

- Ginger

- Fennel

- Lemon Balm

- Horseradish

- Chives

- Echinacea

- Chives

- Chives plant

Chapter 6: How to Grow Vegetables, Fruits, Flowers and Herbs in your Greenhouse

The selection of greenhouse species and cultivars should not be based on single farmer programs but should be the product of an organized program that takes into account agro-environmental restrictions, technological development, and socio-economic opportunities for a particular area. Good farming practices in greenhouse cultivations involve selecting genotypes best suited to a given agricultural context; however, the method is complicated, with a wide variety of solutions to consider. Throughout intensive production systems, such as greenhouse farming, specific fundamental issues need to be addressed before choosing the most appropriate plant or cultivate:

- What to harvest
- When to produce
- How to produce
- Where to sell the product

A farmer has the option of choosing a plant for its high economic value, and designing the most appropriate security, increasing systems and technologies, or selecting and capitalizing on a crop suitable for established farm structures. In most situations, the competition is the limiting factor for intense year-round productions: large yields can be obtained with optimum management of a greenhouse climate conditions, but they may not fulfill consumer criteria (offer does not meet demand). When economic factors (markets) and political decisions (subsidies for certain crops in specific areas) may have a significant impact on crop selection, the emphasis here is on alternatives for different greenhouse agrosystems, most closely linked to the agro-environmental constraints. The option of cultivar often depends on the type of farm: medium- and large-scale farmers may sell their products on domestic and international markets, whereas small-scale farms grow to meet the needs of the family or for minimal income on local markets. Compared to open-field cultivations, greenhouse technologies allow a large number of species to be grown in a specific geographic region as they replicate optimum climatic conditions for certain species in a controlled environment, irrespective of the external environment. The risk/reward ratio is a significant determinant of the level of technology implemented in greenhouse systems that indirectly reflects the current geographic distribution of greenhouse typologies: more secluded (heated, closed and semi-closed) in central/northern Europe; less secluded (cold, open or semi-open) in southern Europe and the Mediterranean. It is an essential factor when choosing plants and cultivars, as various varieties may well conform to specific cultural requirements and protected habitats for the same species. Cold greenhouses and covered cultivations focus on vegetable crops belonging to the families of the Solanaceae (tomato, pepper, eggplant) and Cucurbitaceae (melon, summer squash, watermelon, cucumber) under moderate climatic conditions. Such crops (representing > 80 percent of the protected area in most Mediterranean countries) respond to cold greenhouse conditions and meet local market needs. The popularity of safe farming is attributed to:

- Wide intake;

- Great adaptation to unstable climatic conditions within cold greenhouses due to indeterminate growing habits of the crops; and

- Long growing cycles (more continuous use of greenhouses during the year).

- On the other hand, Leafy determines crops do not embrace the latter qualities and thus may experience bolting control-related problems with effects on yield and quality of the product. To preserve the economic sustainability of the established greenhouse industry and enhance the performance of farms introducing protected cultivations in new areas, crop choice may become increasingly important. Crop choice will identify organisms and genotypes capable of providing different produce typologies, taking account of environmental and economic conditions, crop characteristics and specifications, harmony between crop and microclimate, and soil characteristics and plant-borne diseases, more specifically:

- Consumer criteria

- Environmental comfort

- Economic and social sense

- Consumer gap

- Field-scale

- Production requirements

- Labor requirements

- Climatic conditions

- Security characteristics imply

- Probability of successful climate control

- Soil requirements and soil-borne diseases

The key criterion for market demand for a particular product is a differentiation between common greenhouse crops and other small crops (specialty crops, e.g., squash flowers, or goods are eaten locally, e.g., gombos). In all cases, given the increasing costs of production and the short shelf-life of vegetable products, crop selection should ensure an optimal match between production and duration of shipment to the market. The economic concerns involve the connection between the prices of the commodity and the returns of the farmers. Production costs are not fixed: for example, labor may range from a factor of 1 to 8 in Mediterranean countries. Fertilizers, chemicals, and transport often vary considerably in quality. If growers plan to grow for local markets, alternative solutions such as pick-your-own, roadside markets, or agreements with local grocery stores can be implemented to reduce transportation costs. Such schemes, however, are not accessible in greenhouse agriculture, which relies mostly on organized retail delivery or agreements with supermarkets and supermarket chains. The provision of on-farm (or nearby) cold storage rooms is helpful–also crucial– in maintaining the consistency of perishable goods before transport. There are other essential crop criteria to be addressed in addition to the natural texture of field and shelter (e.g., tunnel depth and height of vertically trained plants). In general, the higher the climatic conditions, the lower the compliance with the most widely utilized indoor shelters in mild winter climes. The labor requirements should be considered, as should the availability of labor during the growing cycle. The time and labor needed for a specific crop should not be overlooked, especially in small (family) fields, and, if necessary, the demand should be measured in advance. Also, some tasks may require different levels of specialization requiring additional investment in training or technological equipment (e.g., hydroponic fertigation units). Protected agriculture can be in a wide variety of situations involving the external conditions. Greenhouses are situated in different climates but with higher concentrations in regions where winter is mild, and places where temperature threats are low; however, the extension to areas with significant climatic risks has taken place. Besides, under protected cultivation in mild winter climates, the characteristics of greenhouse construction and the frequent total absence of active climate control have a significant effect on the microclimate (Baille 2001). Thus, since farmers depend on first crop defense systems, selecting a species that matches the particular climatic conditions while maintaining reasonable control of the growth climate (e.g., tomato vs. pepper) is essential.

Greenhouse manufacturing is an economic sector that is very dynamic and must cope with rapid changes in market trends and consumer preferences. The choice of cultivar is essential for each crop and the typology of specific products. Cultivars that produce fruits with varying characteristics in the greenhouse production system are not valid alternatives that must meet strict production and market requirements. Cultivars for controlled cultivation vary dramatically from those used in open-field vegetable production: they are less vulnerable to environmental restrictions and can, therefore, better articulate their capacity for yields. Depending on the level of technology used in protected cultivation (e.g., cultivars adapted for long-cycle crops), different cultivar-specific requirements may also exist, however. Owing to restricted greenhouse climate control, growth techniques in Mediterranean greenhouses had been focused on adjusting plants to a suboptimal atmosphere. The preference of one cultivar over another can be influenced by a range of factors, and farmers, traders, and customers have different perspectives. For example, possible yields, prolonged harvest period with consistent product quality, and tolerance to biotic and abiotic stresses are essential considerations of farmers. The advent of stress-tolerant cultivars calls for a significant reduction in chemical treatments, environmental pollution, and cost of production, thus providing new opportunities for the application of advanced cultivation methods and organic greenhouse growth. Nonetheless, when introducing resistant cultivars, the durability of the specific resistance under different microclimatic and agronomic conditions must be addressed. Long shelf-life and any features that render the commodity distinctive and highly appreciated (and therefore requested) by customers are essential factors for the trader. The drug has to be simple to use, flexible, with excellent taste and safety products for the user. Cultivar preference would theoretically take all of the above considerations into consideration, but in reality, growers identify different priorities about commodity destination and specific market objectives. It is necessary to choose cultivars that can respect the environmental conditions and technological factors involved in the manufacturing process in specific areas. Recent advances due to rapidly developing breeding technologies have resulted in a substantially broader portfolio of new cultivars with genetic characteristics for improved disease resistance, adaptability to suboptimal temperature and light, and other specific features, such as parthenocarpy and greasing suitability. While the above traits are all significant in greenhouse growth, it is vital to determine their sensitivity in the actual growing area under different conditions. This is not an easy task, as the high rate of reconstruction of the suitable cultivars and the absence of comprehensive agronomic production testing indicate that there are no reliable data to provide useful information to the farmers. Because of the many characteristics that a cultivar is supposed to have, seed and breeding firms are seeking to satisfy market demands and extend the cultivar range. Furthermore, there are legislative, regulatory and qualification criteria for product quality and safety, as well as limits on chemicals used in agricultural production (Leonardi, 2005), all of which increase the pressure for the selection of high-quality cultivars capable of tolerating most prevalent pests and diseases in the greenhouse. Simultaneously, seed companies continue to force their offerings on the market with a consequent decline in germplasm variability and the inevitable loss of essential and useful genetic traits. Systematically organized breeding projects are required to conserve local genetic resources suited to specific environments so that biodiversity can be capitalized, preserved, and maintained.

It is necessary to develop a local screening system for evaluating and testing recently released cultivars in a representative greenhouse region (with funding from local administrations and research institutions), to assist farmers and promote the advancement of vegetable cultivars in parallel with standard practices established by seed and breeding companies (Williams and Roberts 2002). Such an extension program should also provide farmers with technical advice on cultural aspects to reach the yield and quality potential of specific species. The feed-forward-feed-back process between growers, extension programs, and seed companies will build an effective system for maintaining and valuing underexploited genetic capital. There is increasing interest in crop diversification in greenhouse agriculture, more than in other agrosystems, to maintain the economic viability of the existing greenhouse industry and improve the performance of farmers who have planted covered crops in new areas. An essential aspect of the economic survival of covered crops is the discovery of new plants for incorporation into farming systems. Besides the basic requirements of adaptation to cold greenhouse conditions, they should guarantee an economic return that must be competitive with that obtained with other crops. Results of an EU research project in the 1990s, covering many European countries, demonstrated the promise of certain specialty crops, including crops grown on small acres, indigenous vegetables, gourmet vegetables, miniature vegetables and vegetables that are scarce or uncommon in some regions. Throughout recent years, the popularity of specialty vegetables has dramatically increased. There are other new crops (e.g., okra, orach, rocket, asparagus, lettuce) that give satisfactory agronomic results but somewhat limited market demand. Paradoxically, the most critical example of diversification relates to a well-established crop: tomato (La Malfa et al., 1996). In recent decades, new plants have been developed to produce new types of fruit by capitalizing on its intraspecific genetic diversity. Cherry and cluster tomatoes in Italy were quite rare 20 years ago and now account for more than 50 percent of greenhouse growth. For the sustainability of the entire production cycle, crop diversification, obtained by growing new species or varieties and in some cases new cultivars, is necessary. The introduction of new crops may compensate for commodity losses due to unexpected biotic or abiotic pressures, or market fluctuations, and improve the overall resilience of the agrosystems. The use of transgenic cultivars allows adding valuable traits to greenhouse crops is an increasingly important issue in this respect. Although still under consideration, the use of transgene technologies in agriculture to boost the development process's environmental sustainability is a common practice in many nations. It could be approved in Europe in the future. Nevertheless, crop diversification in cold greenhouses in the Mediterranean is unlikely to reach the heated greenhouse levels. Leaving aside the economic factor, a heated greenhouse can be tailored climate-friendly to almost any plant condition. At the same time, in unheated greenhouses, plants may conform to an internal environment that relies on the external temperature. These species ' photothermic requirements should not be too high so that they can be met by simple modifications of internal microclimatic conditions; however, they should not be so low that they reduce or nullify the benefits of the greenhouse environment in terms of productivity, quality, and harvest time. New crops must withstand widely variable thermal ranges daily and seasonally for these environments. The minimum and maximum temperature ranges achieved every day in these environments are often outside the thermokinetic scope, i.e., the biologically acceptable thermal period. This period is not always well established for crops with new candidates. A greenhouse can yield the most significant beneficial effects on plants with a long cycle and infinite production, to enable the more extensive use of a greenhouse. Specific considerations are weighed when picking new crops in addition to the plant characteristics: operational issues (e.g., using the greenhouse during summer rest periods as well) and commercial motives (e.g., enhancing efficiency by increasing the delivery period). Given the substantial interspecific and intraspecific diversity of vegetable plants (hundreds of species in the Mediterranean Basin alone), diversification in a cold greenhouse is therefore very restricted. Based on this study, it can be inferred that, in terms of shelter typology, the characteristics of a candidate new crop for Mediterranean cold greenhouses vary. In comparison, the main requirements for new plants in the Netherlands for heated greenhouses are year-round planting, tolerance to soil and heating crops, high yield capacity, low labor requirements, high thermal requirements (making outdoor cultivation impossible), and high quality relative to open-air goods. All other factors–the cost of production, product quality, and overlap in the production calendar with other open-air crops–are valid for heated and unheated greenhouses.

More than 1,000 species are consumed as "vegetables" worldwide. In greenhouse outputs, there are several origins of new crops:

- plants imported from other countries;

- small species and varieties developed in the past, and now ignored or not routinely grown;

- Cultivars of plants already commonly grown in greenhouses but capable of providing new characteristics to vegetables;

- species to date only produced in the open air; and

- wild species, consumed as vegetables.

- Adapt to agro-climatic and social conditions;

- meet customer specifications; and

- be lucrative and profitable.

- Innovative crops related to traditional ones and able to produce new types of vegetables include cherry tomatoes (20 years ago), beef tomatoes (recently), immature pea pods, small eggplants, small peppers, tiny strawberries, yellow and variegated green bean pods, and yellow courgettes. These should be considered new to certain areas (in the Mediterranean), although elsewhere they might already be well known. The competition is undoubtedly a major driving force in introducing a new seed. Seedless watermelons were a popular product with widespread use. In other instances, a specific product may not be widely distributed, such as gombo (Abelmoscus esculentum). Still, it reacts to very particular consumer demand (in this case from Asia and Africa). New crop success relies on market opportunities. Consequently, diversification could be aimed at producing relatively small quantities of a particular product if it is directed at a specific market. Sadly, the current greenhouse farming systems do not have adequate tracking and knowledge on new crops to create a database to be used as a guideline. This also obstructs further development of these crops and the likelihood of up-to-date cultural technologies emerging.

Conclusively, Species and cultivar selection is a significant factor when considering the sustainability of protected cultivations. While the selection process is complicated, some key aspects can be clarified. The decision is based on a step-by-step approach to understanding competition and goals, followed by a detailed study. This method is focused on the understanding of existing know-how and on the prospect of carrying out experimental activities; it is to be called fluid and, therefore, adaptable to the ongoing development of societal, economic and agronomic circumstances; thanks to a feedback study

Chapter 7: Plants for Year-Round Growing

When you plant your plants in a greenhouse, you can allow them to give you harvest as often as you want to. Plants will only give you a harvest when they are ready to. However, with the process of growing your plants on a schedule, you can make sure that you have some sort of harvest coming in all year long. We will look into how this works and some tips and tricks to help you along the way.

First, let's look into why you would want to have a harvest all year long. If you have plants that can be harvested from all year long, you have fresh fruits and vegetables available to you every day of the year. If you grow enough plants, this could even replace your produce purchases at the grocery store. It will allow your family and yourself to be the healthiest versions of yourself that you can be. It will give you something to look forward to each day, and it will allow you to continue to feel the success of growing in your greenhouse throughout every single season. Having a year-round harvest greenhouse can be a challenging process, and we will look into these struggles below along with the benefits—but it can be a great thing as well.

Next, let's look into how you can make this happen. How can you possibly have a greenhouse that has to products available to you every single day of the year? It sounds like something that would be fairly difficult. In reality, it is a simple process. It requires a lot of work and a lot of planning, but once you get that plan into action, I can be a simple thing to follow through with.

To learn about how you can make this happen, let us look into what we already know. We already know that you can plant in greenhouses all year long. We already know that you can keep your plants alive in your greenhouse all year long and that you do not need to keep planting new plants for each season. Your plants can stay alive. We know that this is possible through the use of heaters and adequate lighting through artificial sources when it is winter, and we know that this is possible through fans and vents when it's hot in the summer. When you have a greenhouse that can be used every season of the year, you can, of course, plant in every season of the year.

No, let's look into what we do not yet know. We do not yet know how you can have plants give you a crop all year long. Of course, you are not going to get a tomato plant to keep producing your tomatoes constantly day after day for years straight. Fruits and vegetables have growing seasons. They have seasons were they grow food and seasons were they prepare themselves to do so. You cannot make an apple tree have apples all year long. You cannot make an orange tree grow oranges all year long. The plants need to have their time to prepare themselves oh, they cannot have food on them every single day.

Because of this, there must be another way to allow you to gain a crop from your greenhouse every day of the year. This other way is by planting your plants on the schedule. When you plant a seed, you know when it will become mature by the number of days it provides you on the back of the packet. For example, if a tomato plant takes 120 days to reach maturity, this will be listed on the back of the seed packet. When you know how long it will take to produce fruit or vegetables, you will be able to count on that plant to produce a crop for you at that time. Because of this, you will then know if you plant a tomato plant that you will have tomatoes in 120 or so days. The same holds for every type of plant. When you plant something, you should be able to tell how long it will take that seedling to turn into a plant that bears food.

Now, if you want to have every month of the year filled with these tomatoes, you will need to plan a harvest for each month of the year. To do this, you will need to pick out that month that you want the plan to be ready, and count back 120 days or however long it takes tomatoes to reach maturity. Once you count back these 120 days, you will find that the day that you need to plant your seed on. Columbus Day, you will probably want to plant many seeds. If you plant many seeds, you will have a better chance of getting at least some of them to survive.

After you have planted your seeds, go ahead and find the next date when you would like a new tomato harvest to happen and do the process all over again. If you want your hair was to happen once a month, you can simply plant the seeds on the first day of every month. Once you have gotten the pattern started, the math will always be 30 days later. Because of this, you can simply plant on one day of the month every month.

If you plant one day of the month every month for a year, you should then have a harvest coming in every single day of the year. As long as you care for your plants in a way that allows them to bear fruit and vegetables, will have your plants set up on a staggering schedule to give you a crop.

You can choose to do this year-round growing with one type of plant or with all of your plants. If you only want carrots year-round, for example, you could simply just choose to keep planting carrot seeds when you want them to grow. If you want all of your plants to have a harvest every day of the year, you will do this with all of your plants. To do this, you might need a bigger greenhouse. If you only have a small greenhouse, you can consider only doing year-round growing with your favorite plants.

Another important factor to consider when growing plants all your robes is that your females need to be ready for every season. If you live in a cold area, you will want to make sure that your greenhouse is winterized and ready for the cold winter. You will want to make sure that your heater is working and that it is running, as well as that all cracks and holes that could be in your greenhouse are covered and are not letting air in. He will also want to make sure that any big jobs are done before winter comes so that you do not have to open the doors or windows for long amounts of time as this can make the air in the greenhouse become very cold very quickly. If you are growing your round and you live in a place that has very hot summers, you may want to be prepared with things like some shades and vents on your greenhouse for air circulation. For the spring and fall, you need to be prepared as well. The preparation for these seasons varies based on where you live—but for the fall, you should be prepared for winter; and for the spring, you should be prepared for summer.

Why do you need to have your greenhouse ready for every season? You need to have your greenhouse ready for every season because you are growing in every season. If you have a harvest every day, that means you are growing every day. This means that your plants need to be alive and healthy every day. To make this happen, your greenhouse needs to be repaired and in the optimal environment for the health of your plants as well as their success every day of the year. This means that you need to take your seasonal preparation and care very seriously. It has a much more detailed approach to this information.

Another thing to consider when you look into year-round growing is that you need to be ready to do a lot of work every single day of the year. When you do year-round growing, you do not have an off-season. You do not have a break in between crops where you do not need to go out into your greenhouse. You do not have a time where you are not doing multiple jobs at once. You are growing seedlings, planting seeds, caring for plants, and harvesting all in the same day. This means that you are around growing can take a lot of your time and energy in ways that typical greenhouse gardening cannot. Of course, for this extra effort, it does provide a lot of added benefits with its increased amount of crop and harvest, but it needs to be a level of work that you are ready for if it is something that you want to consider. This extra work also takes up a lot of extra time. If you want to have a year-round growing garden inside of your greenhouse, you need to make sure that you have enough time to do so. Finding the time to prep for each season, plant seeds, care for your plants, and harvest all at the same time can be challenging. Year-round growing inside of your friend house is a commitment that you need to be all in for if you want even to consider it.

With extra harvests, year-round growing also comes with extra costs. If you want to grow plants year-round, you will be buying many more seeds. You will also be buying much more soil, and maybe even many more trays if you cannot reuse the old ones. You will be using more water well water in your extra plants, and he will be using more light to provide the heat and lighting that your extra plants need. Make sure that you can cover these extra costs if you are ready to have extra harvests year-round growing in your greenhouse.

Another thing that you should know about year-round gardening is it is great for people who want to sell their crops. If you are looking to sell fruits or vegetables, year-round gardening can be a great choice. If you do your gardening and sell your crops, you will be one of the few farmers or gardeners who can sell fruits and vegetables during their offseason. If you can sell fruits and vegetables during their offseason, you will have a huge advantage over your competition. Typically, people miss fresh fruits and vegetables in the wintertime. If you can provide them with you is, you will have a lot of business. You will have a lot of happy customers, and the extra work that you put into your year-round gardening will pay off quickly.

Year-round growing can be hard. Because of this, we want to share with you some pieces of advice. Let's look into some tips and tricks that you can use to make year-round growing easier for you. Our first step is that you should start with a plant. Make sure that you know what you want to do. If you do not have a plan in place before you begin, you are around growing can seem overwhelming. You need to know what types of plants you want to have and when you want to harvest them. You also want to have a plan for where you are going to grow your plants since they take up extra space as well as how you are going to get the extra resources. You may even want to plan out how you are going to have enough time to spend growing all of these plants at once.

Our next tip is that you should make sure you have a large greenhouse for a creative space plan before planning on having a year-round harvest. It is okay if you have a small greenhouse, but if you do have a small greenhouse, you need to be creative with the small space that you have. Look into different shelving units, or even considered growing one set the plants underneath the normal bench with artificial grow lights to maximize your space.

Also, if you are planning on participating in year-round growing, consider asking for help. Ask your friends and family to help you with watering once in a while. Ask your neighborhood children to help you with planting seeds. These are things that your family, friends, and neighbors would probably love to help you with if you asked him. The extra help would also give you the ability to care for plants in a way that you may not be able to do on your own.

Along with that last tip, if you offer some of the harvests to your helpers, they may be much more willing to help. Tell your neighbors that they can take some tomatoes whenever they like if they come over and help water them or help you plant some seeds. If you spread the word that you are helpers will get it back in produce that comes from your garden, you will probably have many more volunteers as well as much better luck getting them actually to come and help.

Our biggest tip for year-round growing is to be prepared. Look ahead at the challenges that you might face. Be ready for what you need to do if you have some sort of greenhouse emergency. Make sure that you understand you will be using many more lights and much more water. Understand that you will be spending a lot of time in the greenhouse. Make yourself comfortable with these facts and even happy with them. If you do these things, it will be much easier for you to grow your plants year-round in a greenhouse.

Even though growing plants year-round in a greenhouse is hard, we want you to find success. We believe that if you follow these tips and tricks and learn all the information that we have shared with you, you will be able to have success at year-round gardening. As long as you have the tools, knowledge, and passion necessary to do this large task, you will have great success.

Overall, it is easy to see that year-round growing inside of a greenhouse is a difficult but rewarding task. It is something that takes extra time, extra money, extra resources, extra effort, and extra dedication to keep up with. Along with all of these things, however, year-round growing in a greenhouse also provides you with added benefits. It gives you harvests year-round. It allows you to have healthy food to put on your table every day of the year. It allows you to plan for what you want to eat and when you want to have it ready. It is a rewarding and beneficial process in many ways. Year-round growing can be a great thing to do—you just need to make sure that you are up for the challenge before you begin.

Chapter 8: Hydroponics in your Greenhouse

The possibility of hydroponic (gardening without soil), has been around since the hour of King Solomon. There are a couple of preferences with hydroponic gardening over conventional gardening - for instance, the pace of development of a hydroponic plant can be up to half quicker than a dirt plant become under similar conditions.

What's more, the yield of the plant is additionally greater! The explanation behind this is the plants get their sustenance took care of straightforwardly into their foundations from supplement rich water. Since this water is so high in supplement content, the plant needn't bother with huge roots to scan for nourishment. What's more, since the plant exhausts less vitality in developing roots it has more vitality accessible to be beneficial over the root line! Hydroponically developed vegetables are solid, enthusiastic, and reliably dependable. This type of gardening is spotless and incredibly simple, and it requires next to no exertion.

Hydroponic gardening is likewise valuable to the earth. For instance, hydroponic gardening utilizes significantly less water than soil gardening because of the consistent reuse of the supplement arrangements.

Furthermore, fewer pesticides are important in hydroponic yields - they are not as essential. Also, topsoil disintegration can't an issue since hydroponic gardening frameworks utilize no topsoil.

How precisely does a hydroponically developed plant get its nourishment - sustenance it ordinarily gets from the dirt? All things considered, these supplements come in fluid or powdered blends and can be bought at a hydroponic inventory store. What's more, similar to soil, hydroponic frameworks can be prepared with natural or concoction supplements. In any case, you should realize that a natural hydroponic framework can be extensively more work to keep up since the natural mixes have an inclination bunch.

Hydroponic frameworks are regularly arranged as aloof or dynamic. A functioning hydroponic framework moves the supplement arrangement with a siphon. A detached hydroponic framework depends on the slender activity of the developing medium or a wick.

In a detached framework, the supplement rich arrangement is consumed by the medium or the wick and went along to the plant's underlying foundations. In any case, a drawback with this technique is that they are typically excessively wet and don't supply enough oxygen to the root framework for the best development rates.

Hydroponic frameworks are likewise portrayed as recuperation or non-recuperation. In recuperation frameworks, the supplement arrangement is re-coursed for reuse. In a non-recuperation framework, be that as it may, the supplement arrangement can't.

You might be uncertain of whether to purchase or assemble a hydroponic framework. If you have a 'designing psyche' and need to manufacture one, consider getting one first just to get acquainted with the inward activities. Purchase a framework which doesn't cost a great deal of cash. It will give you a superior comprehension of how hydroponics functions and the hands-on experience can merit the expense of the framework as you will have the option to reuse the parts when you choose to construct one.

Hydroponics gardening is a famous and developing interest and many are seeing this as fun, exciting Free Reprint Articles, and simple to begin.

Although there is a wide range of sorts of hydroponic frameworks, they all work utilizing similar essential strategies. As a matter of first importance, hydroponic developing frameworks permit plant roots to come into direct contact with supplements and oxygen, which are both fundamental to plant development, without utilizing soil. Rather than soil, some hydroponic frameworks utilize different sorts of developing media, as stone wool, mudrocks, coco coir, vermiculite or perlite to offer help for a plant's underlying foundations. In other hydroponic frameworks, similar to those that fuse hydroponics, no developing media is required by any stretch of the imagination.

Concerning plant supplements, these are conveyed legitimately to plant roots through a water-based, supplement rich arrangement. This arrangement can be applied to the roots utilizing a few different techniques. A portion of these techniques incorporates, however, are not restricted to, the roots being suspended in the supplement arrangement, for example, the profound water culture strategy or the roots can be clouded with the supplement arrangement, which is utilized in hydroponics, a.k.a. fogponics or mistponics.

Notwithstanding, abundant supplements and oxygen are not by any means the only components that assume a fundamental job in plant development. Light, alongside supplements and oxygen, must be accessible for plants to assimilate, as it is a basic segment in photosynthesis. Much like the supplement arrangement, legitimate measures of light can be conveyed to plants developed hydroponically in a couple of different ways. Some hydroponic frameworks are open, depending on normal lighting, while different frameworks depend on artificial lighting to furnish plants with satisfactory measures of light.

What is hydroponics utilized for?

Hydroponics is rapidly picking up prevalence in places where customary cultivating just isn't an alternative. In huge urban communities, there is next to zero access to agronomically reasonable land. In any case, hydroponics fills in as an answer for the issue of constrained developing space. Hydroponics tackles this issue because it tends to be executed anyplace. This applies to enormous scope, business ranches, however little family gardens also.

The mix of hydroponics and vertical homesteads has allowed numerous enormous urban areas the chance to approach crisp privately developed produce. This is the reason in numerous enormous urban areas hydroponic ranchers are purchasing up unused structure spaces of every kind imaginable and utilizing them as vertical-ranch building spaces. In huge urban communities, vertical ranches have been worked in spaces, for example, void distribution centers and old delivery compartments. Many accept these kinds of hydroponic homesteads can positively affect urban networks by giving crisp produce and supporting neighborhood nourishment supplies.

For what reason is hydroponics so famous for indoor gardening specifically?

Developing plants inside with hydroponics permits gardeners to make a garden in their home regardless of whether they have a constrained measure of room. Notwithstanding having the option to develop plants in a limited quantity of room, indoor hydroponic gardening has a few advantages. One especially reasonable advantage is that hydroponic gardening is considerably less messy than soil gardening. Also, indoor gardens can be a practical wellspring of great produce all year, given the ecological conditions are kept ideal.

Indoor hydroponic gardens have a few other auxiliary advantages too. By developing plants inside, gardeners can control numerous parts of the developing condition. This incorporates the control of plant sicknesses and bugs. Last, however surely not least, an advantage that may not be often considered, is that plants developed inside guide in cleaning the demeanor of different poisons and discharge oxygen once again into the encompassing indoor condition.

What are the benefits of hydroponics?

One of the most perceived advantages of hydroponics is that nourishments developed in indoor hydroponic frameworks are not liable to developing seasons. Indeed, nourishment developed along these lines can be created all year in significantly less time. Not exclusively can crops be developed in each season, the yield in hydroponic homesteads is twofold the production yield of soil-based ranches because the development cycle is continually restarting. Yield can't higher, yet numerous hydroponic ranchers guarantee that the nature of the hydroponically developed product is a lot higher.

Hydroponic ranches not just beat customary homesteads underway; they don't have a portion of the significant hindrances that accompany soil-based cultivating, especially in the territory of asset utilization. Albeit hydroponic frameworks rely upon water and water-based answers for performing appropriately, they use around one-twentieth of the measure of water utilized in customary gardening and cultivating.

This is because in most hydroponic frameworks the water is often reused and reused, restricting the general sum that is required. Also, hydroponic homesteads don't deliver run-off. In conventional cultivating, run-off can prompt the corruption of the general condition. In any case, with hydroponic homesteads, water can be reused on various occasions.

Notwithstanding utilizing significantly less water, hydroponic homesteads don't require a similar measure of upkeep that customary ranches do. For instance, hydroponic frameworks don't generally require pesticides because hydroponic plants are developed in controlled situations and therefore are not defenseless to soil-borne sicknesses, vermin, or organisms.

Hydroponic homesteads likewise require considerably less work than customary ranches because they are in minimal spaces, often as midsection elevated levels. Therefore, gathering and replanting is a lot simpler with hydroponic frameworks (no burrowing or weeding required!), making the general upkeep of hydroponic frameworks insignificant.

What are the drawbacks of hydroponics?

Although the benefits of hydroponic cultivating enormously exceed those of conventional cultivating, the weaknesses have shielded hydroponic cultivating from being executed for a bigger scope. The greatest impediment of hydroponic frameworks is that the underlying set-up costs are exceptionally high.

Some little, locally situated hydroponic frameworks can be assembled generally economically, yet huge scope cultivating tasks can accompany a sticker price that runs into a huge number of dollars. This is because enormous hydroponic cultivating frameworks require significantly more specific gear and specialized information than is required in customary cultivating.

Enormous hydroponic homesteads additionally require consistent supervision and checking. The measures of supplement arrangement, lighting, and oxygen that plants get are painstakingly observed by experts. Moreover, hydroponic cultivating is vulnerable to something customary grounds ranches are not: power blackouts. In case of a force blackout, plants can dry out and harvests can be lost.

Force utilization by huge scope hydroponic homesteads is additionally a worry. Numerous indoor hydroponic ranches rely upon artificial lighting to furnish plants with their light needs as opposed to depending only on the sun. Be that as it may, numerous producers accept that if these disservices can be settled, hydroponic frameworks could be a monetarily suitable option in contrast to conventional cultivating.

Chapter 9: Maintaining A Hydroponic System

Hydroponic gardens need to have proper care and maintenance, or they will not produce healthy plants. Not only do they need to be constantly cleaned, but various maintenance checks need to be carried out to make sure the system remains functioning correctly.

A faulty drain or a leaky pipe or switch could do serious damage to a hydroponic garden as most of the systems rely on their equipment and parts to work smoothly.

Cleanliness

To stop the buildup of algae, mold, and fungus or to stop attracting pests, keep the growing room as clean as possible.

Equipment should be flushed and cleaned at least twice a month to maintain water levels, stop algae growth, and ensure that no pests are lurking about the system.

To stop pests and various fungal growth, growers should always make sure their hands are clean. Hands should be kept washed especially after handling anything that was dirty or in contact with a harmful substance.

Do not let old fallen leaves, stems, fruit, produce or growing media or even pots or discarded trays lie around the growing areas. Rather throw out any debris or broken items, and wash and pack away any unused equipment.

Wash all equipment after use and only reuse a growing medium if it can be reused and it has been thoroughly washed and sterilized. All growing mediums, whether old or new, should be thoroughly washed before being used as not to contaminate the grow pots, grow trays, and the reservoir.

Keeping the growing area and equipment clean cuts down on the chances of infestation and development of frustrating diseases that are a nuisance to get rid of.

Nutrient Solution

The proper nutrient solution for the plant type and system type should be used at the correct ratio of solution to water.

Only use good quality nutrient solutions with an organic base. Advance nutrients are only required should there be a problem that needs to be fixed, such as a nutrient deficiency in a plant.

The nutrient solution balance should be checked regularly especially is it is a recovery system where the solution is being continuously recycled.

Make sure that the solution is flushed and completely refreshed regularly and that there is no salt buildup since this is very acidic and toxic to the plants.

Watering

Watering is done in many different ways and is delivered to each of the hydroponic systems differently.

Make sure the water is always fresh and checked regularly. Algae is a common problem, as is nutrient build up in the system. An oxygen pump should be installed to ensure the water is being well hydrated and to keep the water fresher for longer.

Water solutions can come from the tap, drain systems, or rain collection tanks.

Watering can be on a continuous flow basis or set by a timer that switches on and off at different intervals during the day.

If possible, a person should always have a backup water solution available in case of an emergency and their primary watering source is unavailable. Some plants are very sensitive to their watering schedule and even a few minute's downtimes and a missed watering schedule can cause some damage.

Reservoir Temperature

The water in the reservoir should be around 65 to 75 degrees Fahrenheit, which is the basic room temperature. Water that is either too hot or too cold can damage the plant's root systems and their leaves.

The reservoir should be topped off with water to keep pH and nutrient levels constant. Change out the water regularly.

Humidity

Different plants and hydroponic systems need the humidity to be on different levels. Some thermometers can measure the humidity and temperature to ensure that the plants are comfortable. Keeping an optimum level does not encourage the growth of unwanted diseases and fungi.

Make sure plants that love the hotter temperatures get enough humidity by giving them a regular misting spray. This will help to keep the humidity constant for the plants that do not like too much humidity.

Inspect the Equipment

The equipment should be thoroughly inspected regularly.

There are a lot of things that can go wrong in a hydroponic system, especially with the equipment. And the best way to troubleshoot is to try to avoid as many equipment malfunctions as possible.

The best way to inspect equipment to keep the entire system in mind. When doing the inspection starts at one point and work your way through your system.

Start with the reservoir and all the systems that are dependent on it.

•Water feeding pipe

•This should be thoroughly checked for crimps that may not be feeding the solution correctly.

•Nutrients build up in the pipes so they may need thorough flushing out or replacing.

•Check for any blockages in the pipe.

•Check for any holes or leaks that could deter the flow of water pressure in the pipe.

•Check for any algae or mold that may be growing in or around the pipe.

•Determine if it may be time to replace the hoses.

•Give them a good cleaning if they are still viable.

•Nozzles and hoses

•Check the nozzles that feed the root systems, sprinklers, or misting systems.

•When last were they changed?

•Check for blockages or leakage.

•Check any joins and washers for leaks.

•Check for sediment build-up, algae, or mold growing in or around these attachments.

•Give them a good cleaning if they are still usable.

•Drain siphons and hoses

•Check the drain pipes for blockages

•When last were they replaced?

•Check for leaks.

•Check for algae or mold growing in or around these pipes.

•They may need to have a good cleaning as part of the system maintenance.

•Check the reservoir water pump

•Test the pump

•Make sure it is still working correctly and pumping the water at the optimum flow.

•Check that all pump attachments are not leaking air.

•Check the reservoir

•Check that there is no buildup, algae, or mold growing on the reservoir.

•Check for any leaks.

•Make sure the water is at the optimum temperature for the hydroponic system and plants.

•Check that any air pumps are functioning correctly and adequately oxygenating the tank.

•Make sure any oxygen stones do not have unwanted algae or mold growth on them

•Growing trays

•Make sure the growing tray(s) do not have any leaks in them.

•Make sure the growing tray(s) are clean and have not unwanted algae or mold growing on them.

•Clean off any nutrient build-up and make sure the trays are clean.

•For a closed system, the trays must be given thorough flushing out.

•Growing pots

•Check that each of the pots is still intact and not broken.

•Replace any that are not functioning correctly.

•Make sure any growing medium is clean and does not have any unwanted algae or mold growing on them that could upset the plant's natural balance.

•Lighting equipment

•Check that the bulbs are still functioning correctly.

•Check that the lighting is still adequate for the environment.

•Check the timers are working correctly.

•Clean any residue off the lighting system.

•Temperature

•Make sure that any thermostat is working correctly and that room temperature is normal.

•Check that the humidity is correct for the growing environment.

•Check both the temperature and humidity thermometers to ensure that they are still working correctly.

•Ventilation

•Make sure that there is adequate ventilation in the growing room.

•Not enough ventilation can cause mold.

•Check that all fans and cooling systems are working correctly.

•Support Systems

•Check that any hanging supports for the plants are working without causing the plant or system any undue stress.

•Make sure that the environment in which the hydroponic system is housed offers the correct infrastructure for the system to function correctly.

•Make sure the plants are all supported and planted correctly to ensure a successful infrastructure.

•Tools

•Are all the gardening tools in working order?

•Are they cleaned?

•Are there any that may need to be replaced?

Look at Your Plants

Make sure you keep a vigilant check on your growing plants. Measure their growth rate, root growth and when they are ready to harvest.

This gives a person a good measure of how the next batch should perform and something by which to determine if the growing medium, solution, or systems structure may need to be changed or optimized.

The plants must also be checked to make sure they are getting enough nutrients, they are growing as they should, and there are no pests or other infestations. A lot of growing problems and deficiencies can be caused by various infestations. Some are easy to spot, others may take more of an experienced eye, but as a gardener gets to know their plants they will come to instinctively know when something is wrong.

Look for the signs in seedlings such as slow growth, looking sad and droopy, white fluffy stuff growing on the leaves, etc.

Take the time to look over the plants; do not just rush through it.

If there is an outbreak, you will need to go through the entire growing area right away.

Spending time with the plants in a hydroponic environment can also be quite good for the mind and spirit. Plants and running water are rather therapeutic and can reduce stress, anxiety and ease tension.

Change One Thing at a Time

If you are wanting to change or expand your system, do not try and do it all at once.

Before rushing out and buying expensive parts, why not try a bit of DIY and try to make it yourself. Or at least look around to see what you have available before rushing off to spend more money on an item you do not need.

Hydroponic systems are not only flexible and versatile in what they can grow or how they deliver their solutions, but they can also be easily adapted to suit the grower's needs and lifestyle.

There are so many great DIY ideas on how to create the perfect hydroponic garden online these days that it is well worth a try. The money you save building the system yourself can be better spent on plants, growing media, or nutrient solutions.

To keep a system simple and working for you, think carefully about an upgrade or addition.

Chapter 10: Common Greenhouse Problems

Problems can pop up in greenhouses no matter how well you treat your plants. Do you not feel bad if any of these problems pop up? Simply look back at this information and figure out how you can solve the issue quickly and effectively. We will look into the problem in detail, who learn why it occurs, and learn how to fix it. Let's get started.

First, let's look into what to do if you get bugs in your greenhouse. Is there something that you would think of dealing with outside? You do not want to need to deal with them inside of your greenhouse. The first reason is that you are already in a structure—you should not have to deal with something like bugs. The second reason is if bugs are in your greenhouse, it is not like they're simply going to be like when they are outside. If bugs are in your greenhouse, they probably think that they are there to stay. You will need to do something to get them out of your greenhouse. They are not going to fly away like they were outside.

Let's start by looking into why bugs get into greenhouses. If there is any space that allows bugs to get into your greenhouse—like a crack or hole or even vent or door that was open for a few seconds—bugs can get in. Bugs go inside greenhouses because they know they're filled with plants and because they want to pollinate them. Bugs can also go to clean houses just to simply explore. Other bugs are looking for plants to eat. You do not want these latter bugs in your greenhouse. You do not want your plants to get eaten by anyone except for you.

Next, let's look into some ways that you can prevent bugs from getting into your greenhouse. One of the easiest ways to prevent getting bumped into your greenhouses is to look at the things that you are bringing inside. If you are bringing inside a plant, make sure there are no bugs in it. If you are bringing in new soil, make sure you do the same. Anything that you bring in should be checked to ensure that there are no bugs that could hurt your plants on them.

Another thing that you can do to avoid getting bugs in your greenhouses to make sure that they do not have a way in. Make sure that all cracks and holes are filled. Also, if you have a fence, you could consider putting a screen on them. You can put screens on the windows as well. You can also make sure that when you come in and out of the greenhouse, you do so quickly and you do not leave the door open.

It is also a good idea to not plant anything around the outside of your greenhouse. If you put plants around the outside of your greenhouse, these plants can attract bugs. If you attract bugs next to your greenhouse, they will likely know that there are plants inside and they will likely find a way in. You want to keep all of your outdoor plants far away from the greenhouse to avoid this happening.

Now, let's look into what to do if you already have bugs inside of your greenhouse. In an outdoor garden, you might reach for the pesticides. This is not a great idea inside of a greenhouse not only because they are toxic chemicals but because in such a small space they can be a hazard. One helpful way to catch bugs inside of your greenhouse is to use bug traps like tape. You can hang out tape all-around in your greenhouse, and it will not affect your plants. It will, however, catch the bugs that you do not want to be there. You could also consider making sure to get rid of anything that will attract bugs. For example, make sure that there is no standing water available in your greenhouse. If your bugs are not attracted to anything inside of your greenhouse, they may leave. If you are having a hard time with bugs in your greenhouse, you could always ask a professional exterminator for help.

Something that can be problematic is your greenhouse disease. Many different things can cause diseases in your plants. These diseases can come from mold, bacteria, and viruses. Greenhouse diseases can be some things that are hard to beat. Let's look into some ways that you can prevent these diseases from occurring in your greenhouse.

What is the most important thing that you can do to prevent disease in your greenhouses? It is to sanitize. You want to make sure that you sanitize everything after you use it. You will need to sanitize 2, trays, and even shelves. If you do not sanitize your tools, it increases your risk of spreading disease inside of your greenhouse from plant to plant. This is because if one plant had a disease and you used a shovel to scoop it out and throw it away, and then use the same shovel in another plant, the new plant would probably get the disease as well just from being touched with the same shovel. The spread of disease in plants inside of greenhouses is similar to the spread of disease in humans. If you stay clean, you will have a much better chance of not spreading diseases.

You allow someone to watch your humidity and make sure that you are greenhouse does not get overly humid. If your greenhouse is too humid, mold and fungus are likely to grow on your soil. If these grow in your soil, your plants will get the disease because of them. Mold and fungus can also spread very quickly and easily. It is something that you want to avoid having in your greenhouse.

When watering your plants, you will want to make sure that the tool does not touch your plant's insurgencies, and you will also want to make sure that the water does not splash while you are watering. If water splashes from one plant to another, it can spread disease. Because of this, you will want to use a tool for watering that does not allow water to splash. You will want to use the tool that has a light spray that soaks into the soil and does not splash at all.

Another thing that can help prevent disease is to make sure that plants have adequate space between them. If your plants are too close together, they will be touching each other, and this can cause them to spread diseases to each other. If your plans are spaced apart, when one plant becomes diseased, the ones around it will not be touching it and will likely not become diseased along with it. Sometimes, it can be a hassle to spread plants out in your greenhouse because it feels like a wasted space, but it is better to waste space than to allow all of your plants to become sick.

One last thing that you can do to protect your plants from disease is to look at them every day. Walk around your greenhouse and look for signs of disease. Look for things that look out of the ordinary. If you see a plant that does not look healthy, consider taking it out of the greenhouse and quarantining it for a while. This will allow you to tell if the plant is infected with the disease as well as keep it away from other healthy plants to make sure that they do not catch a disease if it has one. With this process, it is helpful to know what plants look like when they are diseased. If the plant has mold or fungus, you will probably be able to tell right away. If it has mold growing in the soil or mushrooms growing in the soil, it means that it has mold or fungus. This is one of the easiest diseases to tell if your plant has. Another sign that your plant has a disease is that it has large, raised brown lumps on its leaves. These lumps typically mean the plant is sick. Plants that seem to be dying even though you are taking great care of them can be diseased as well. Any plant that is showing signs that are not normal should be taken away from your healthy plants just in case a disease is present.

Next, let's look into what to do if a plant is serious. If you see that a plant is diseased, make sure you take it out for a greenhouse right away. This will help to make it not infect other pants. Also, you should look at helping it right away—especially if you can save your plant when all signs of the disease are gone and bring it back to the greenhouse. If not, at least, you only lost one plant and not your entire greenhouse to a disease.

If you take the necessary precautions to make sure that diseases do not enter your plants and take it seriously when a plant is looking unhealthy, you should have success in keeping this problem away.

We are going to look into what to do if you look at some plants in your greenhouse and see that their leaves are turning yellow. Yellow leaves are a common occurrence and plants, but they are not a good sign. There's something that you want to deal with and help right away. If you do not help a plant that has yellow leaves, it will likely die from the cause of the discoloration. Many different things can cause yellow leaves in plants, so let's get started in figuring out what they are.

The first thing that can cause yellow leaves in plants is something called moisture stress. Moisture stress is when a plant gets either too little water or too much water. If a plant is not watered often enough, it will have both dry soil and yellow leaves. If a plant is watered too much, it will have wet soil as well as possible mold or fungus growing in it and yellow leaves. It should be pretty easy to tell the difference between these two problems. You will know if you have been watering your plant a lot or if you have forgotten many days in a row. Even if you do not know this information, you will be able to tell by the moisture level in the soil. If your plant has yellow leaves that have too much water or too little water, it is very easy to fix. Simply make sure that you give your plant the accurate amount of water starting at the moment that you notice the yellow leaves. If your plant is under-watered, you can consider giving it a water soak. To do this, you can soak the plant in water in assessing or in a tub for anywhere from a few minutes to a few hours. If your plant is overwatered, consider giving it some period without water. Once it is dry again, however, make sure you water it normally. Do not wait too long to water it again because then it could turn yellow from not being watered enough.

If you find yellow leaves on a plant and you know that you have been giving it the correct amount of water, think about how much light it is getting. If a plant does not get enough light, its leaves can turn yellow. If you have a plant with yellow leaves and you know that it has not gotten enough lately, considering moving it to a location that it will get more sun in. If you do not have a space in your greenhouse available where this plant and get more sun, you will need to give the plant adequate artificial lighting to help it survive. This again is an easy fix. If you find a plant with yellow leaves and it needs like, once you give it light its leaves should correct themselves, and it should go back to being a healthy plant.

Another reason why a plant can have yellow leaves is that the temperature for the plant is wrong in the environment that it is in. If your greenhouse is too hot or too cold, the leaves of plants can turn yellow. Most likely, if this is the cause, many plants in your greenhouse will have yellow leaves and not just one. This is because all of the plants are experiencing the same temperature, not just one. That is one good way to tell if yellow leaves are caused by temperature. If a plant in your greenhouse is too hot or too cold, you simply need to fix the temperature in the greenhouse to allow it to go back to normal. Once the plant reaches the temperature that it wants to have, it should fix itself, and its leaves should start growing green instead of yellow. This again is an easy fix if you notice it while the plant is still able to be healthy.

If you believe that the environment for your plant is completely perfect and that you have been wondering it well, the yellow leaves may be caused by something else. The last cause for yellow leaves that we will look into is plant nutrition. If you have been treating your plant perfectly and it still has yellow leaves, this could be the cost. Typically, you will be able to tell when plants are turning yellow from a nutrition problem because the yellow will appear in strange patterns. It will not just be a yellow leaf for half of the yellow leaf. The yellow may come in lines, or it may appear only in the veins of the plant. Usually, when a plant has a nutrition problem, it is either caused by having too much fertilizer in the soil or by the plant having a disease. If you have been treating your plant and have not put too much fertilizer in it, consider separating the plant from the others to make sure that you are not allowing it to spread disease.

Overall, there are a lot of causes that can cause a plant to have yellow leaves. Luckily, most of them are very solvable and very easy to figure out. When you look at your plants and consider what it means and what it is not getting, you will be able to figure out why it is yellow, and you will be able to fix it quickly.

The last issue that we are going to look at is the occurrence of dying plants. Dying plants are typically caused by one of the greenhouse problems that we have already mentioned. They are typically caused by greenhouse problems that go on seeing, however. Because of this, if you keep a good eye on your plans and watch their symptoms, you should not have to deal with dying plants.

If you have plants that have bugs in them, for example, you should be able to notice the bugs right away. Every time you go into the greenhouse, you should see bugs flying around, or you should see bugs crawling on your plants when you inspect them closely. You may even notice that your plants are being eaten by these bugs. These signs are hard to miss. However, if you miss them, you will start to see dying plants in your greenhouse.

The same is true with diseases. If you have these plants in your greenhouse and you do not notice them, you will eventually have dying plants instead. If you do not catch the disease in time, the disease will spread. They will kill the plans that they have already gotten too, and they will spread to even more plants. If you do not notice diseases in time, they could wipe out your entire greenhouse. This would be a tragedy. It would take all of your work and bring it to a loss. If you do not notice diseases in your greenhouse, you will eventually have dying plants in your greenhouse instead.

Once again, the same holds the yellow leaves. Yellow leaves usually have easy fixes as we read about just now. However, if you do not notice yellow leaves and you let the plants continue to suffer and not get what they need to survive, you will eventually have dying plants instead. You need to notice your yellow leaves when they are only on a few leaves of the plant. If you notice that your plant is covered in completely yellow leaves, it is probably too late to save.

Conclusion

The greenhouse is a system of change and management of the environment that allows plants to grow in climates and seasons that otherwise do not fit well with their growth. It is an environment in which you can control the factors that promote the growth of plants. Factors such as heat, humidity, ventilation, sun, etc. These factors and many others determine the quality and quantity of their performance.

The construction and design of a greenhouse should be made based on these factors because they can determine the optimal greenhouse performance.

Make sure the site has easy access to the water, electricity and other necessary public services. High, stable soil is needed to avoid unnecessary water accumulation. Find a place where there is decent ground for growing plants or the potential to grow. Expandability must also be considered.

Greenhouse plants are exposed to many pests and diseases. In addition to the particular problems of plants, some many pests and diseases attack plants in greenhouses. Therefore, health and control of pests must be carried out. Insects such as aphids, whiteflies, leaf miners, etc. affect performance in a greenhouse.

The list of pests above may seem painful or even frightening, but remember that this is an exhaustive list of major pests. It's unlikely you'll get them all. You can go years without it. It is better to be prepared. If you know how to recognize parasites and fight them, you've won the battle.

Many problems with pests and diseases caused by the greenhouse effect can be greatly reduced by only observing a good cleaning practice. Always remove all old plant materials and greenhouse composts, and whenever you use a knife to cut or remove damaged plants, always clean these tools with a good garden disinfectant. Also, always keep very strong chisels and pruners, as this will reduce damage to plants, which can cause infection or pest attack.

The area around a greenhouse should be kept relatively free of weeds and plant material that can carry pests. This can be done with winter fabric or a plant covered in a barrier at least 10 feet wide around the structure. Preferably, an area with grass should be maintained beyond this area.

Pests often enter the main entrance of a greenhouse because it is the path of least resistance. A lock entry is essential in greenhouses equipped with fan and pad ventilation systems. An airlock can only be obtained by installing a room that locks the door of the greenhouse.

Greenhouse gardening offers many benefits that go beyond the benefits of conventional gardening. One of the main benefits of growing greenhouses is that they offer a longer growing season. Temperatures do not vary so much in a greenhouse because solar radiation is trapped within the enclosure, which retains heat in the structure. The growing seasons can be extended even in cold climates.

With a greenhouse, you don't have to worry about the weather because everything is covered. Even if it is raining outside, you can garden and stay dry. You have the opportunity to grow a variety of plants when using a greenhouse. It allows people to experience exotic plants that are not found in the area.